Also by Helen Singer Kaplan

Progress in Group and Family Therapy with
Clifford J. Sager, M.D.

The New Sex Therapy

The Illustrated Manual of Sex Therapy

Helen Singer Kaplan, M.D., Ph.D.

MAKING SENSE OF SEX

The new facts about sex and love
for young people

Drawings by David Passalacqua

Simon and Schuster
New York

Published by Simon and Schuster
A Division of Gulf & Western Corporation
Simon & Schuster Building
Rockefeller Center
1230 Avenue of the Americas
New York, New York 10020

Manufactured in the United States of America

1 2 3 4 5 6 7 8 9 10

Library of Congress Cataloging in Publication Data
Kaplan, Helen Singer, date.
    Making sense of sex.
    Includes index.
    1. Sex instruction for youth.   I. Title.
HQ35.K34   613.9′5   79–15054
ISBN 0–671–25131–7

To my Mother
and to Phillip, Peter and Jenny

Contents

Why I Wrote This Book and What It Contains for Parents and Teachers

This book provides frank, explicit, comprehensive, and up-to-date information about the biology and the psychology of the sexual experience. One of its objectives is to organize and to make sense out of the enormous amount of new data on human sexuality, a topic that has suffered from incredible ignorance, confusion and misinformation.

But more important than the factual information is our concern about the sexual and emotional well-being of our young people. The facts are, of course, important, but no matter how completely and brilliantly conceived, they are of limited value in human terms if our attitudes toward sex are negative. Negative attitudes are more potent than ignorance in stunting the sexual and emotional lives of so many of our children. Information will merely inform, but it takes "heart"—an encouraging, reassuring, and positive attitude—to convey to the young person the message that sex is a natural and beautiful human function. This message is the most active ingredient in the prevention of problems, in enhancing a person's ability to love and to enjoy a sexual relationship.

A Book for Young People

This book is written primarily for adolescents, who really need the facts and also the reassurance that their sexual feelings are normal. This is the time of their lives when sex and love become very important to them, when they begin to experience, and have to deal with, urgent and unfamiliar erotic feelings. This is a critical time in sexual development, a time of profound vulnerability when painful sexual and psychological problems can be spawned. It is also a time of great opportunity when a healthy capacity to enjoy sex and love can begin to emerge. Unfortunately, young people in our society often enter this critical period ignorant, confused, and guilty about sex. They often harbor erroneous beliefs which frighten them and impair rather than foster their growth and development in this important area. It is my hope that their sexual development can be enhanced, and some problems prevented, by the accurate information and the constructive and positive messages about sex and love that I have tried to convey in this book.

The New Facts

Much of the scientific information about human sexuality that is presented in this book has been accumulated very recently and may be unfamiliar even to professionals. And this is not because sex is very complicated or difficult to study. On the contrary, sex is a relatively simple human function. But for a long time sex was not regarded as a natural biological function by our society. Sex was thought of as sinful, evil, and dangerous, and the study of sex was taboo in hospitals, laboratories, and even in schools. For this reason, until very recently, it was extremely difficult for legitimate scientists to investigate sexuality. Thus the study of sex was neglected by the scientific establishment. Doctors knew much more about the physiology of other bodily functions such as digestion, respiration, and nutrition and were capable of offering effective treatment for illnesses of a non-sexual nature. Every doctor knows how to treat a sore throat; but very few know how to help if you can't have an erection. Until this last decade, we were ignorant about the human sexual response. We didn't understand the causes of sexual problems very clearly, and our treatment of the sexual difficulties from which millions of people suffer was not very effective.

Fortunately, our society's negative attitudes about sexuality are changing. Responsible people are reevaluating our long-held prejudices and are concluding that reproduction and sex are natural biological functions, and that many of our attitudes are irrational and actually destructive to both scientific progress and to the quality of human life. So within our lifetime, for the first time in Western history, sex has become a legitimate topic for study. These studies have taught us what the sexual response of men and women is really like. We have also become increasingly aware that the unconflicted development of a young person's sexuality is important for optimum mental health. Finally, we are learning how to prevent and how to treat sexual disorders.

Among the contributors to our new knowledge about human sexuality, Freud, Kinsey, and Masters and Johnson are outstanding.

Sigmund Freud, the creator of psychoanalysis, studied the causes of mental and emotional problems. He found that the roots of neurotic problems of adults often lay in the problems experienced in childhood. As he studied childhood development he made the startling "discovery" that small children have sexual feelings. Previously, babies were thought of as "innocent"; that sexual experience began at adolescence. Now we know that erotic feelings and behavior commence at birth and undergo a definite developmental sequence, like all other human functions. Freud went further; he warned that a child's erotic needs should be respected and that he should not be made to feel guilty or frightened about these. He taught us that many psychological problems have their roots in the sexual conflicts which we instill in our children from a very early age on. Specifically, he called our attention to the fact that excessive or harsh suppression of childhood sexuality produces unconscious conflicts which may cause the person to become neurotic and psychologically crippled for his entire life. Interestingly enough, Freud's views on childhood sexuality were received with outrage by his medical colleagues and also by Viennese society. He suffered much criticism for raising our consciousness about the fact that little children have sexual feelings.

Another pioneer was Alfred Kinsey and his associates, Pomeroy, Gebhard, and Martin. They questioned thousands of American males and females, of all ages and from varying socio-economic-religious backgrounds, about their sexual habits. Actually the Kinsey *Report* would not have been particularly remarkable if Kinsey had asked people what they ate. No one would have paid the slightest attention. But since their inquiry was about the taboo subject of sex, it caused an uproar. Actually Kinsey's most important finding was that most normal people enjoy sex in various ways throughout their lives and do not seem to be damaged thereby.

Decades later the courageous innovators, William Masters and Virginia Johnson Masters, studied human sexual responses in the laboratory for the first time in history. Again, there is nothing really unusual about observing a biological function under controlled laboratory conditions. We are always taking X-rays of the stomach during digestion, recording brain waves while a subject solves a mathematical problem, analyzing urine samples to see how well the body handles sugar. But no one had dared to study the genital organs of men and women and how they function during sexual arousal in the same scientific way until Masters and Johnson summoned the courage to do just that. Over a period of ten years they observed, measured, and studied some 14,000 sexual acts in a specially built laboratory. Masters and Johnson also devised special instruments which enabled them to record previously unknown sexual reactions. For example, they invented a transparent plastic, penis-shaped instrument which contained a light and a tiny camera and allowed us, for the first time, to find out what happens inside a woman's vagina during penetration. Masters and Johnson studied the biology of intercourse, of masturbation, of sex during menstruation, the sexual responses of old people, the sexual responses of homosexuals, and the sexual behavior of patients who have sexual problems. These studies yielded invaluable information. For one, they confirmed Kinsey's conclusion that sex causes no physical harm. Indeed, the subjects usually found the erotic experiences in the lab enjoyable.

Most important, Masters and Johnson described the normal physiology of the male and the female sexual response which had been a mystery even to doctors. Their studies also exploded many myths which had arisen from a combination of ignorance and prejudice. They showed, for example, that sex changes but need not stop as a person ages. They recorded the sexual activity of persons in their eighties. They also demonstrated that women enjoy sex as much as men do, if not more, and that the trigger point for the female orgasm is in the clitoris, and not in the vagina as had been previously believed.

The data accumulated by these researchers, and by others as well, have provided us with the facts which were needed to finally construct a clear and rational concept of what the sexual response of men and women is all about and what causes sexual problems.

And in addition to extending our biological knowledge, the new data on human sexuality is being applied to the development of effective new treatment techniques. These are urgently needed because millions of persons suffer from sexual problems. In the past, only a small percentage could be cured by the old traditional medical or psychiatric treatments.

The new facts about sex will *not* by themselves cure a sexually disabled patient. But a therapeutic approach has emerged, which is based both on our new, and rational, understanding of sexual physiology and our traditional knowledge of medicine and psychiatry. This new sex therapy, which uses a combination of sexual techniques and psychotherapeutic skills that deal with emotions, now offers hope to many persons who were beyond help in the past. These new developments and concepts are described in this book in simple and clear language appropriate for the young person.

Sex and the Emotions

I am often asked by parents, "What shall I tell my child about sex?" "How much should a thirteen-year-old know?"

Of course accurate information is important, but it is really not all that crucial exactly *what* you tell your children. It is *how* you tell them, the tone of your voice, your *emotions,* the non-verbal messages you give them. What is in your *heart* counts much more than what is in your head.

Again, the attitude underlying this book is that sex is a natural function and that feelings of shame, guilt, or fear are irrational and damaging to the individual and to his relationships with others.

Sex and love are exceedingly important elements of the human experience. The capacity to love and to experience sexual pleasure greatly enriches our lives. In fact, when those aspects of ourselves are crippled and constricted, we never attain our full human potential. Love and sex are very sensitive and can be stunted or enhanced by the emotional attitudes of a child's family. Therefore love and sex, like other potentially constructive human functions, should be encouraged by a youngster's family and school and community. And this must start from the beginning of life. Sex does not suddenly appear at adolescence or at the time of marriage. Adult sexuality is the end product of the long, natural, developmental process which begins with birth. Sex is not unique in this respect. All adult functions are the product of a long and epigenetic process of development. Growing up entails learning and practicing, and trial and error in all areas: tennis, social skills, cooking, studying, and so on. To develop skill and confidence in anything, the youngster has to be allowed to rehearse in the form of play, games, and fantasies. How well he develops in these areas is in large part shaped by the feedback he gets from the important persons in his life.

Language development is not so different from sexual development. Information and emotional messages are both important influences in shaping a youngster's linguistic skills. And language, like sex, can be stunted or enhanced by the child's experiences. A baby makes sounds, babbles, first just for the pleasure of it. Baby hears and enjoys his own noises. Then sounds get responses from people he loves. Mother smiles when baby coos. "Did you hear him say Ma?" she exclaims with pleasure. Then facts are introduced. Certain sounds become associated with objects and with the gratification of needs. The child learns the power of words. He plays with words, then with sequences of words, then with sentences. As his brain develops, more complex neural patterns are established which provide the biological infrastructure, the apparatus for linguistic capability. Now he begins to use the playful sounds in different ways, to express concepts and ideas. And he is constantly fed facts and encouraged by emotional messages that language is O.K. Talking and writing are rewarded. He goes to school; there he increases his vocabulary and polishes his syntax until he develops into a mature and perhaps creative orator. And throughout the entire sequence he receives the loving encouragement of his family. From them he receives positive and negative feedback. Responsibility in the use of language is just as important as encouragement. He is allowed to speak, but he gets the message that he is not to take over, to talk all the time, nor to interrupt or to lie or use words to hurt others. Limits are set. However, in families where intellectual and expressive skills are valued, he is basically encouraged to develop his language skills. His parents convey pride. "Isn't he clever!" "He got an A on his book report!" In some lower-class families where language skills are not encouraged, the information is scanty, and the emotional message is, "No one cares, don't bother, don't speak up," with devastating consequences for a youngster's intellectual, emotional, and social development.

Many of these same elements operate in sexual development. Appropriate limits are very important. Youngsters should be taught that sex is a major area of vulnerability. They should be encouraged to be sensitive to the feelings of others, not to use sex destructively or exploitively. But there is good reason to believe that unless a youngster receives the message, from the day he is born, that his penis is just as beautiful as the rest of his body; that sexual pleasure is O.K.; unless he is encouraged to develop his sensuous and erotic skills, he may at best never reach his full human potential, and at worst develop serious sexual and emotional problems.

Authorities have estimated that sexual problems are the most prevalent medical complaints in the world, more common, in fact, than the common cold. This is shocking but not surprising if we consider that sexuality is very delicate and that it tends to be dealt with uncomfortably and even harshly by many families of our society. Even the most loving and sensitive parents often handle the sexual development of their children poorly. Their own conflicting feelings about sex tend to be translated into negative messages which tell the child: "Don't," "It's not nice," "It upsets Mother," "It will hurt you," "It will hurt her." These messages may not be consciously recognized by the child, but they nevertheless can influence his behavior for the rest of his life. These negative feelings about sex contrast with the loving and conflict-free attitudes which govern caring parents as they foster and shape other important functions such as eating, sleeping, defecating, walking, talking, and so on. Just think what would happen if we were brought up in a society in which attitudes about food were as negative as our attitudes are about sex! What would happen to you if your mother's face reflected painful discomfort each time you took a bite of food; if you had to eat by yourself in the dark; if you were given the message that your mouth is repulsive; if you were not allowed to talk about food or admit you were hungry; if you heard sermons about the evil of eating and the sins of yearning for meat or sweets; if you could never share a meal with another person until you were in your mid-twenties and married; if even fantasies about food were laden with guilt! It is safe to guess that in such a society stomach ulcers, appetite disturbances, bizarre oral desires, diarrhea, and constipation would be quite as common as sexual problems are today. And these guilty, fearful, emotional attitudes about sex are instilled by caring, loving parents with the best intentions.

A little boy touches his penis because it gives him pleasure.

His mother pushes his hand away, and even though she does not say a word, her body and her face communicate pain and disapproval. He enjoys the sexy feeling but does not want to upset this person he loves. He has gotten his mother's message that sex is bad. At this moment his conflict about sex begins. Parents do not behave this way because they are destructive. Most parents love their babies; they wish them well and want to protect them from harm. Unfortunately, they believe erroneously, that childhood masturbation is harmful, and it upsets them to see it. For they, too, are products of and prey to the social forces which have attached an irrational stigma of guilt and fear to sex.

Explicit and open as it is, this book is not meant to promote irresponsible or compulsive sexuality. On the contrary, it conveys my belief that the pendulum has probably swung too far in the direction of genital performance to the exclusion of emotional satisfaction. Sexual freedom should not be confused with promiscuity, mechanical sex, or with demands for a national standard level of genital performance.

In every revolution there are some casualties and errors, especially in the beginning, when established values are being altered. In the long run, the sexual revolution—or as I prefer to call it, the humanization of sexuality—will bring immense benefits to men and women. However, at this early stage, perhaps too much pressure has been put on young people to experience intercourse prematurely and/or too often and with the wrong person. Sex has become a status symbol to some. There is too much emphasis on the genitals and not enough on caring. Sex is used competitively, like an athletic performance. Performance pressure is just as destructive to the full development of the human potential as its opposite—abstinence from sexual pleasure in order to avoid the pain of guilt and fear.

When we are sexually liberated we should be able to experience and enjoy sex without fear of guilt or shame, and only if, when and how we are authentically moved to do so. Sex is not enjoyable if a person does it because she thinks it is expected by her peers or by her date. It is only satisfying if you are moved by your true desires and if it feels good and right. A young person should be equipped with accurate information and a guilt-free positive attitude toward sex so that he can be *free*—free to experience sex or free to abstain without guilt or shame or pressure.

Contents

There are many "sex education" books which provide excellent information about human reproduction, but they tend to avoid or at any rate make short shrift of sex. But young people need explicit information about sex. Because youngsters seldom have a realistic picture of lovemaking, they tend to develop peculiar misconceptions and misleading fantasies. For this reason, normal sexual intercourse is described in the first chapter of this book. The description is followed by a discussion intended to correct some common myths about sex that young people absorb from the pornographic material with which they are inundated.

The following chapter deals with fundamental reproductive biology. Sex is viewed from an evolutionary perspective. There are detailed descriptions of the genital organs of males and females, and just enough information about the structure and functions of the reproductive organs to help the reader make sense out of the material on sex. This is followed by a chapter that describes the three phases of the male and the female sexual response: desire, excitement, and orgasm. The similarities and differences of male and female sexuality are explained here.

With this material, the reader has the foundation required to understand the sexual problems discussed in Chapter Four. Young people often wonder if their own sexual feelings and experiences are O.K., and they tend to worry excessively should they have sexual problems. They need information and reassurance. Many people are ashamed about their sexual difficulties and therefore avoid seeking help. Therefore sexual problems must be presented with an optimistic and nonjudgmental attitude which makes it easier for a person to seek help or advice. A person should feel as free to discuss his sexual health as he does other aspects of his health. In this chapter, some of the difficulties people experience in functioning sexually are described along with brief explanations of homosexuality, bisexuality, and gender problems. Young people raise many questions about these subjects and often need reassurance.

Next, there is a chapter summarizing reproductive physiology, including basic concepts of ovulation and menstruation, sperm production, conception, and pregnancy. The next chapter, on birth control, presents the controversy about the moral issues of preventing unwanted pregnancy. Various forms of birth control methods are discussed in terms of their advantages and their risks and disadvantages. Following is a chapter on some of the more common sexually transmitted diseases.

The six sexual ages of man and woman are described in the penultimate chapter. Psychosexual development is reviewed from infantile sexuality through menopause to old age. Gender differences in the sexual aging process are discussed. Also included in that chapter are discussions of masturbation and the meaning of sexual fantasy; topics most young people have questions about. And the book ends with the most important issue of all: love.

Discussing Sex with Young People

I am aware that some responsible and constructive people will have misgivings about providing adolescents with explicit sex information and about conveying an attitude which regards sexuality as a natural and beautiful human function. While I respect and understand these feelings, I obviously do not share such misgivings. My view, the opposite, is that problems can be prevented and lives enhanced if our children's sexuality is fostered with the same thoughtfulness and loving care that is devoted to the other aspects of their development; that children should be provided with accurate and sensible information, and that they should feel they have the right to ask for help with their sexual problems.

My experience as a clinician, educator, and mother of three wonderful children has taught me to trust in the basic decency and good sense of the young. They use knowledge in constructive and responsible ways and have much to teach *us* about morality and humanity. I have seen only good come from rearing youngsters in an environment in which accurate information about sexuality is available and in which sex is considered to be a natural human function. On the other hand, in my clinical practice, I have seen many tragic problems produced by ignorance and by the linking of love and sex with guilt and fear. When erotic and affectionate human feelings are alienated from the total personality, painful sexual inadequacies can result. And, even more tragic, the alienation of the sexual aspects of ourselves results in general feelings of tensions and inadequacy. Defenses are then erected against such intolerable feelings, which distort the entire personality, and worst of all, erode the person's ability to trust and to love and to enjoy the experience of human intimacy.

Even when they are well informed and convinced that it is beneficial, it is often difficult for parents to help their children learn about love and sex because they are uncomfortable with this subject. I remember my own, well meaning, loving mother's total course on sex education, delivered with great embarrassment when I was about twelve: "When a man gets hard down there, you should leave immediately." She did a much better job of teaching me how to prepare delicious food for parties.

The discomfort generated by sex gets in the way of clear and honest communication with our children. It is so much easier to teach them how to cook or ride a bicycle or how to acquire good study habits. And yet a parent's or teacher's failure to communicate comfortably and clearly constitutes a negative message that adds to their confusion. So I hope that this book will serve two purposes: To present the facts about sex in a useful and sensible way, and to convey a clear and positive message that sex is O.K. and that people have a right to enjoy sexual health.

MAKING SENSE OF SEX

Chapter 1

MAKING LOVE
Reality and Myth

A man and a woman walk together. They hold hands. Their eyes express affection. She hangs on to his every word. He finds her comments charming. The sounds of their voices, the animation on their faces, their posture, their touch, all express delight in being with each other. It is obvious that theirs is not a business association. They are lovers, emotionally and sexually attracted to each other. When they are alone together he kisses her. She responds. First with closed lips, then their tongues explore each other's mouth. They kiss slowly, again and again. His hands begin to explore her hair, face, and neck. His hand gently touches her breasts. Her hands also caress his hair and neck and chest. Slowly they begin to undress. He kisses each part of her skin as it is revealed. Her hand touches his penis, which is now erect inside his pants. He unzips his fly. She runs her fingertip over the surface of his penis and then kisses it lightly. They lie together gently kissing and caressing and delighting in each other's bodies, slowly but with rising excitement. His hands touch her back and buttocks, her arms, her neck, her breasts. He kisses and sucks her nipples and she moans softly. His fingers gently play with her pubic hair and touch and tease her labia, which have grown moist. Her hands fondle his penis and testicles in return. Finally, his fingers, moistened by her lubrication, play around her clitoris. First slowly, but as she responds his pace quickens. Her breathing becomes more rapid. "Now?" he asks. "Oh, yes," she says. He enters her and thrusts—slowly at first, and then at a quickening pace. She too is thrusting in rhythm with him. "Are you ready?" "No, but you go ahead, please." They quicken their pace, he shudders and groans with pleasure as he climaxes. The couple lie quite still for a minute. Then he withdraws his penis and gently holds her in his arms while he stimulates her clitoris with his finger until she too tenses and writhes and experiences her climax. Afterward, the couple lie together and slowly caress each other's bodies with their fingertips.

Myths about Sex

It could have gone a bit differently. She could have climaxed during intercourse. I chose to describe the "taking turns" way of having orgasm because many people mistakenly believe that it is abnormal for a woman to need direct stimulation of her clitoris in order to reach an orgasm. Actually, only approximately 30 percent of sexually active women climax on penile penetration alone. The majority of normal women have orgasms only when the clitoris is stimulated. It is important for both men and women to understand that clitoral responsiveness is a normal sexual pattern and highly enjoyable as long as it is not considered "second best." Far too often lovemaking is spoiled by a compulsive striving for mutual orgasm or by heroic attempts to have the female partner climax during penetration. A woman's inability to have an orgasm during intercourse may lead to an unnecessary sense of failure for both her and him. Some perfectly normal women are not coitally orgastic and even though she greatly enjoys penetration, and even though the couple practice the most skillful lovemaking techniques, and even if he is the most attractive guy in the world, and even if the couple is deeply in love, such women will not climax during intercourse. The couple should not be disappointed by this because sex can be highly enjoyable and gratifying even if you take turns climaxing. A woman who needs clitoral play to climax can be a great sex partner and she and her partner can enjoy sex immensely. However, "coming together" is, of course, a lovely experience for both partners and if it is possible to attain this one might wish to try to learn how to do it. Some women are initially not orgastic on penetration and later become so after they are more experienced. There are also sex therapy techniques which can help some women to become "coitally orgastic," if this seems important to the couple. These will be discussed in Chapter Four.

I had mixed feelings about describing lovemaking in such detail here—some people might object to it—but it is important to have a realistic view of what sex is all about, and to try to dispel some of the myths and false beliefs which abound about this topic. So I painted this word picture of normal sexual intercourse because in our society such information is not easily available. You don't get the opportunity to watch normal sexual behavior, especially in a gentle affectionate relationship. And the subject of sex is so loaded with emotion that many parents do not talk about it at all. So you can't observe it, your parents don't explain it to you, you can't ask a teacher about it. Unfortunately, as a result, your sexual information too often comes from ignorant and uncaring sources: from boys boasting to less experienced boys, from pornographic films and books which picture sex as mechanical, exploitive, and crude. Men are often shown as sadistic aggressors and women as subhuman sex objects. The ideal male is pictured with a perpetual erection and as eternally ready to have intercourse with any available female, no matter how he feels about her. All he wants to do is "score." The female is a seductress ready to exploit the man's sexual desire in exchange for money or power, and she is also his victim. Gentleness, caring, and intimacy—the most important elements of a satisfying lovemaking experience—are not included in the street picture of sexuality.

Another myth in our society is that the male is the perpetual sexual aggressor who does all the pursuing, while the female is the constant victim who must wait to be asked. The male must always initiate sex, or he is liable to feel "unmanly," while the female is expected to remain passive lest she be considered "ballsy" or aggressive. But these are unrealistic models. Both men and women have sexual desires and either should feel free to initiate a romantic experience, and either may *not* be interested in having sex at any particular time. A normal virile male may not desire sex with every female he encounters. And this is true of normal females also. No one has a perpetual hard-on or becomes aroused all the time.

A related misconception is that the male is always active and the female passive in bed. The male is "supposed" to take responsibility for the lovemaking process. It is his job to arouse himself and his partner. She is to lie there and allow herself to be stimulated. Nonsense. Both partners share the responsibility of making the sex act enjoyable, and either can enjoy being passive and being pleasured, or taking a more active role in stimulating the other. Many couples enjoy taking turns giving and receiving.

The popular literature, porn movies, and erotic magazines tend to glorify the joys of casual sex, of "swinging," of instant sex with strangers. There is no doubt that some people do enjoy such experiences. But for most people sex is best when it is experienced with someone you like and trust and can talk to. When two people are attracted to each other and respect each other and want to please each other and are sensitive to the other's desires, then sex can be really great. If you are having sex with a stranger, you might be so afraid of being rejected if you don't perform well and please your partner that you cannot abandon yourself to your own pleasurable feelings and passions and this can make sex a performance rather than a pleasure.

Another myth is that the genitals always work and that sex is always pleasurable, as it was in the opening scene. This is only true if both partners have no problems and are relaxed. But occasionally a perfectly normal person may get upset during lovemaking. Negative emotions do disturb the sexual response, no matter how attracted you are to your partner. This is a frequent happening when sex occurs between people who do not really know and trust each other, and can't communicate honestly.

Another myth is that if you don't function sexually you are very "sick." Not so. Of course some people do have serious sexual hang-ups but most of the time sexual difficulties are caused by simple situations that can easily be cleared up. Most sexual difficulties, such as coming too fast or not having an erection right away or not feeling much in your vagina, are temporary and will go away if you just relax and try again next time under calmer and more sensible conditions.

The sexual myths which have sprung up in our society are unfortunately perpetuated by the media. Believing them may be harmful to your sex life and your self-esteem.

Some Reasons for Temporary Problems

A great barrier to abandonment and sexual pleasure is the fear of rejection. This results in "performance anxiety." Sex should be a pleasure, not a performance. One should not judge oneself during lovemaking. One should be relaxed enough just to "let it happen." Males are just as afraid of rejection as females, but sometimes for different reasons. They fear being rejected if they do not have rapid erections or if they don't control their orgasms. Some worry that they are not skilled enough to be able to give their partner pleasure. Actually, if a woman cares for a man, his sexual performance is not all that important. Men are also apt to feel anxiety if their partner is not responsive, even though it may be her problem.

Women are also afraid of being rejected for poor "performance"; to them this usually means not having an orgasm quickly enough to keep pace with the man. Women are also worried about their physical appearance, about the beauty of their face, breasts, or figure. Physical appearance may be an element of your attractiveness, but personality and emotional maturity and sensitivity and warmth are far more important. Remember even really ugly people can have great sex lives and get married.

A woman may feel anxiety if her partner does not want to make love or if he loses his erection. She may see this as a reflection of her desirability. Most fears of rejection are unfounded in reality and brought on by a poor self-esteem. The kind of security that permits sexual abandonment is possible only when one feels so good about oneself that one does not worry about being rejected.

Another obstacle to sexual pleasure is guilt. If a person has been taught early on that sexual pleasure is wrong, he or she may have problems fully enjoying the sexual experience later in life.

Fear of pregnancy and of venereal disease is another obstacle which may prevent a person from fully enjoying sex. These are not myths but are realistic fears. If you have intercourse without protection you may indeed become pregnant and unwanted pregnancy is a tragedy. And if you have sex indiscriminately you could contract a sexually transmitted disease which may be dangerous and unpleasant. Your best protection against these fears is to be well informed and take reasonable precautions. There are two chapters later in this book, one on birth control and one on sexually transmitted disease, which explain the problems and offer some advice.

Male–Female Differences

In the scene that opened this chapter, did you notice that the man's and the woman's responses were different in important ways? These differences have to be understood by both partners for successful lovemaking. As most young men do, the man in our scene became excited quite rapidly. He attained an erection in a matter of seconds and was ready to enter the woman's vagina and climax. But he did not do this. If he had, lovemaking would not have been pleasurable for either. Women, epecially when they are young, tend to become aroused at a slower pace and to be penetrated while one is not aroused is usually not a pleasant experience. So her lover slowly kissed and caressed her and when he sensed she was excited, he asked her if she was ready to be entered.

Women tend to become aroused when they are gently touched, without hurry or pressure. A male, especially when he is young, enjoys fondling but does not need it for arousal. A skilled lover will caress the nongenital skin areas of the woman's body first, and only after she seems to respond will he stimulate the erotic areas, which are the nipples and the vulva. Some areas of the body are especially sexy and these are called "erogenous zones." People have different erogenous zones. Some find the ears particularly exciting, others become aroused when the inside of the thigh is caressed, while some are particularly turned on by having their neck kissed.

At any rate, the skillful lover will not stimulate the most sensitive area of all, the clitoris, until his partner is highly aroused. Clitoral stimulation is irritating to most women unless they are already excited, but the clitoris is the seat of women's sexual pleasure and not the vagina, despite myths to the contrary.

And how does a male know where his lover's erogenous zones are, how to stimulate her, when to touch the clitoris, when to penetrate, when to come? He doesn't. Not without experimenting. Not without communicating with his partner. Neither does a woman, for that matter. Men's responses are more visible, but still men vary greatly in their sexual desires. Every person is somewhat different in sexual preferences and pace, and no person really can guess what the other is feeling. It is each person's responsibility to let the partner know, gently of course, where "one is" sexually and what feels good and what does not, what one desires and what is unpleasant, when one is ready for what. Often a woman is initially too shy to ask and tell her lover that she needs more time or that she wants him to stimulate her clitoris. And men may be too proud and too timid to ask. Each somehow feels that the other "ought" to know. But this is wrong. The only way to synchronize the differences between the male and female sexual responses, and the only way to develop a happy and satisfying sexual relationship, is to communicate your desires and your dislikes, man to woman as well as woman to man. You have to take responsibility for communicating because neither of you has a crystal ball. He *can't* know what you like if you don't let him know. This is not to say that lovers should be selfish and demanding and only concerned with their own pleasure. Indeed not, it is just as important to learn what excites your partner as it is to teach him what you like. If you are confident and if your relationship with your partner is secure and trusting, you should be able to communicate your sexual likes and dislikes with comfort. If you don't trust each other enough to be candid, you probably should not be making love to each other in the first place.

First-Time Anxiety

Sex can be great the first time, but often the honeymoon is a disaster. It takes some good experiences before one becomes confident and skillful enough to really enjoy it. Unfortunately, unsuccessful first sexual experiences may have a negative rather than a positive effect on a person's later sexual development.

Sexual responses are delicate, and they are easily disturbed by fear or worry. Almost everyone has some degree of stage fright when he or she is about to experience intercourse for the first time. And that is too bad, because the first time can be a very important influence on later sexual adjustment. If one feels very frightened, lovemaking cannot be successful, and that can be very discouraging, especially if one has no one with whom to talk it over afterward. In fact, the first time may be so discouraging that the person may avoid sex for a long time, and then be plagued by fear and doubt the next time he or she tries. Avoidance only makes things worse because it reduces the chance of doing better next time. A man may fail to erect because he is frightened, or he may climax too soon, perhaps even before entering the vagina. A woman may at first feel discomfort or no pleasure in intercourse. Such unfortunate experiences give rise to doubt and fear, which cause another failure, giving rise to more doubt and fear, and so on and on, escalating into a true sexual problem or dysfunction. This pattern is commonly seen in the histories of adults who seek help with their sexual problems. Often they were poorly prepared for their initial sexual experience, their honeymoon turned out badly, and this started a chain of fear and failure.

Communication

One of the ways to avoid a bad first experience is to have the experience in a good, trusting, communicative relationship. Such a relationship provides psychological security for both partners and protects against the emotional effects of failure. Intercourse will not be abrupt and demanding but will follow a period of enjoyable pre-coital sex play. Then, even if all the reflexes do not work right, the sexual experience will not be a total disaster. At least you can talk about it together sensibly and without hysteria. This way you can learn and pave the way to more successful sexual experiences. When two people trust each other, and are gentle with each other, and don't "awfulize" or overreact to failure if the genitals don't work perfectly each time, they reassure each other and learn and grow together.

THE BIOLOGY OF SEX

Once upon a time there was no life on this planet. No animals, no plants: only rocks and water, and molecules of chemicals dissolved in water, floating mindlessly under the energy-giving rays of the sun. Then one day a miracle happened: A combination of molecules came into being which had the capacity to reproduce itself! Life had begun. The first form of life was relatively simple. It consisted of short strands of amino acids, too small to see with the naked eye. They had assembled themselves out of the oxygen, nitrogen, hydrogen, and carbon molecules which floated about in the sun-warmed waters of the young earth. But small though they were, they had a remarkable quality: They could, and they "wanted to," select more molecules out of the sea and use these to make strands of amino acids whose molecules were arranged identically with their own. And they did just that: they replicated themselves again and again, for millions of years. Sometimes an amino acid strand made a tiny "error" and produced a strand whose molecules were ever so slightly different from its own. This new form reproduced offspring like itself. In other words, the offspring inherited the new trait. And these infinitesimal molecular differences added up through the millenniums, through the countless reproductive cycles which have occurred since life began, have produced the vast array of life which we have on this planet today.

We still have simple self-replicating bits of protein. These are called viruses, and they still steal materials out of the solution in which they exist—in this case living cells—to reproduce themselves, very much like our ancient amino acid ancestors did. For nature never discards a successful life form, it merely adds on new and more complex forms. So in addition to viruses we now have the great spectrum of animal and vegetable life, creatures of incredible complexity and variety which fill every nook and cranny of our ecology.

We have birds that can fly and live in trees and eat insects, and insects that can crawl and hover and fly and help fertilize plants; fish that can swim and eat plankton and be eaten by other sea and land animals, and finally we have man, whose brain is so complex and sophisticated that he has the capability to comprehend and to manipulate the very process of life itself.

This incredible process by which life was transformed from virus to man is called evolution. And evolution is based on reproduction; that is, on a continuous chain of offspring, some of which carry and express small genetic changes.

Not all changes are constructive, of course. Some are disadvantageous to the survival of the individual. But some changes fortunately are adaptive, and these constructive changes enable offspring to compete successfully for survival with "less fit" individuals. The "fittest" survive to produce again, and eventually give birth to species who are even more "fit."

These changes which shape the evolution of life are produced by alterations in our genes. Genes are bits of protein which contain the recipe for creating a new individual exactly like, or just a tiny bit different from its parent. Genes are located in the chromosomes in the nuclei of our cells. They do their work by making specific enzymes which catalyze specific biological reactions. We have about 48,000 different genes and each gene is responsible for some functional or

The Double Helix

The nucleus of each living cell contains material called DNA (deoxyribonucleic acid), which can reproduce itself and which enables cells and whole organisms to reproduce themselves in turn. DNA consists of two chains of neatly arranged chemicals that determine just what substances will be produced by the cell. These two chains are connected to each other by chemical "rungs," forming a ladder-like structure. They are wound around each other in a configuration that has been called the "double helix." When DNA replicates itself, the two chains unwind and come apart, and each one produces a new partner chain from material available in the cell. The double helix may be thought of as the ultimate unit of reproduction.

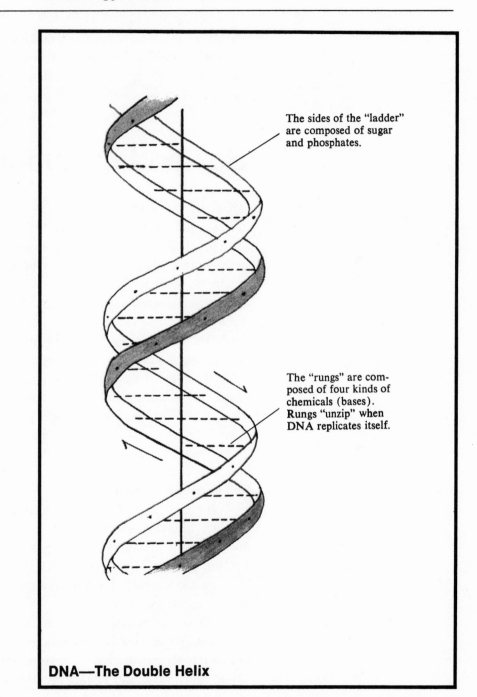

The sides of the "ladder" are composed of sugar and phosphates.

The "rungs" are composed of four kinds of chemicals (bases). Rungs "unzip" when DNA replicates itself.

DNA—The Double Helix

structural characteristic. Genes make your eyes brown or blue, make you six feet tall or five feet short, make you highly intelligent or dull, give you a large or small penis, determine the size and shape of your breasts, bless you with a calm and even disposition or burden you with intense mood swings, and also make you male or female!

Sex and Evolution

There are many ways in which life can replicate itself. The amoeba, for example, simply splits in half. Other organisms "bud." These forms of reproduction have a disadvantage from an evolutionary point of view, in that the parents merely replicate themselves. Their offspring retain the same genetic material and therefore remain pretty much the same from generation to generation. Each amoeba looks the same and behaves the same because it has the same genes as the one before it. Probably today's amoeba is very much the same as his original ancestor several millions of years ago. The only changes that can occur from this kind of asexual reproduction are the products of mutation, which are accidental changes in the chromosomes caused by cosmic rays and chemicals. This is a slow process. Only simple forms of life reproduce asexually. Evolution would probably have stopped at a primitive level if it were not for the development of sexual reproduction. So, incredible as it may seem, if it were not for sex we would still be amoebas and algae!

Higher forms of life reproduce sexually. This means that they produce offspring which contain a mixture of genetic material from two different individuals. This process increases the probability of creating new, more complex, and hopefully "better" progeny, because they are the product of a combination of new and different genes, not just a mere replication.

Sexual reproduction requires the development of two genders—male and female—each of which contributes half of his or her genetic material to their issue. The details of this reproductive process are interesting. Each male and female produces special reproductive or germ cells, but these are different from the rest of the cells of our body. They are haploid cells, which is to say they contain only one half the normal number of chromosomes a cell needs to live.

For example, the cells in the rest of your body, which are called somatic cells—they are the cells in your eyes, skin, heart, liver, brain, and so on—contain 23 pairs or 46 chromosomes. The genetic material in all your millions of somatic cells is identical because they came from the same original fertilized ovum which was your beginning. The human germ cell, however, which is called sperm in the male and ovum in the female, contains only a single set of 23 chromosomes. When sperm and ovum fuse, a new cell is created with a full set of 46 chromosomes.

The same principle is true for all organisms which reproduce by the union of male and female. Different animals contain different numbers of chromosomes in their cells. Whatever that number might be, let us call it **A**. All the cells of the body of that animal contain **A** number of chromosomes, and the germ cells contain $\frac{A}{2}$ or one half of **A**. Because they are incomplete, germ cells die very quickly, but if they should meet another germ cell while they are still viable, they unite, and the whole **A** number of chromosomes is again reestablished. This combined cell does not die, but on the contrary becomes extremely active and forms a whole new individual.

When a male haploid germ cell fuses with a female haploid germ cell, fertilization takes place. The new fertilized cell starts to divide rapidly and grows to reproduce a whole new organism which contains a novel combination of the genetic material from both parents: 24,000 genes from mother and 24,000 genes from father.

Sexual reproduction poses some interesting problems. For one, male and female germ cells must get together to produce offspring. Two, the offspring must be taken care of so it can reach maturity and reproduce again. Through the millenniums, as organisms became more complex, they took longer and longer to develop into maturity. During the immature development period, the young are vulnerable and need special protection if they are to survive.

Comparison of Somatic and Germ Cell Formation

This is a simplified drawing showing the difference between the reproduction of a body or somatic cell—mitosis—and the formation of a germ or reproductive cell—meiosis. Somatic cells are produced when an individual grows or when tissues have to be replaced after an injury such as a cut. The germ cells are produced only in the testes and ovaries, while somatic cells are found in every part of the body.

Notice that all cells, even germ cells, start out as somatic cells and have a whole or diploid set of chromosomes. The creature whose cells are shown in the diagram has four chromosomes, or two sets of two. During mitosis the chromosomes duplicate, line up, and separate, producing two daughter cells that are identical to the original. Specifically, two daughter cells are produced, each having four chromosomes, or two sets. On the other hand, in meiosis, the chromosomes also duplicate, but during the first meiotic division, the cell splits before the duplicated chromosomes have separated, with the result that each new cell has double chromosome pairs (chromatids). The second meiotic division results in four daughter cells, each having only one set, or one-half the number of chromosomes—a haploid

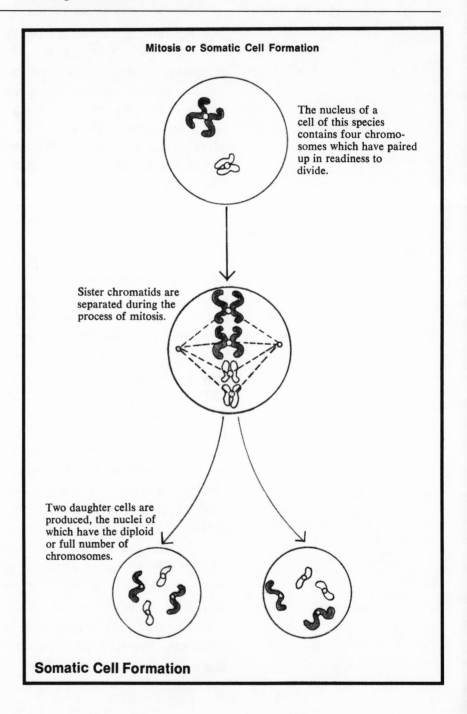

Mitosis or Somatic Cell Formation

The nucleus of a cell of this species contains four chromosomes which have paired up in readiness to divide.

Sister chromatids are separated during the process of mitosis.

Two daughter cells are produced, the nuclei of which have the diploid or full number of chromosomes.

Somatic Cell Formation

number. You might recall that the nuclei of two haploid reproductive cells must fuse to produce a fertilized cell which reestablishes the correct number of chromosomes for that species.

Sperm and ova are the reproductive cells of males and females respectively. Although sperm and ova are similar in that both have a haploid number of chromosomes, the process of spermatogenesis (sperm formation) and oogenesis (ovum formation) is somewhat different. Four sperm are produced by one parent cell or spermatogonium, while only one mature ovum survives from each oogonium. Three of the four resulting daughter cells donate their cytoplasm or cell material to the surviving ovum. The other three contain only nuclear material and are discarded as polar bodies.

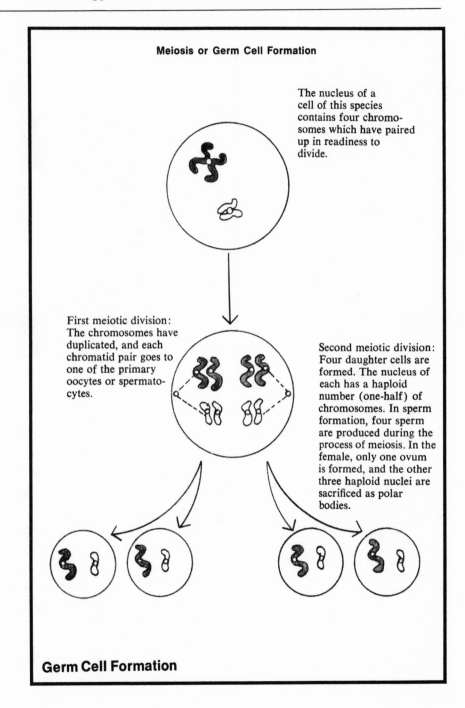

Meiosis or Germ Cell Formation

The nucleus of a cell of this species contains four chromosomes which have paired up in readiness to divide.

First meiotic division: The chromosomes have duplicated, and each chromatid pair goes to one of the primary oocytes or spermatocytes.

Second meiotic division: Four daughter cells are formed. The nucleus of each has a haploid number (one-half) of chromosomes. In sperm formation, four sperm are produced during the process of meiosis. In the female, only one ovum is formed, and the other three haploid nuclei are sacrificed as polar bodies.

Germ Cell Formation

Fertilization

This drawing is taken from a photomicrograph showing the moment of fertilization. The sperm, carrying in its head the nucleus which contains one-half or the haploid number of chromosomes, penetrates the ovum which in its nucleus also contains a haploid number of chromosomes. After penetration the two nuclei will travel toward the center of the ovum and will fuse, reestablishing a diploid or complete number of chromosomes. From this single cell a whole new individual with its millions of diverse and specialized cells will form. One-half of its genetic material (chromosomes) is contributed by the father via the sperm and the other half by its mother via the ovum.

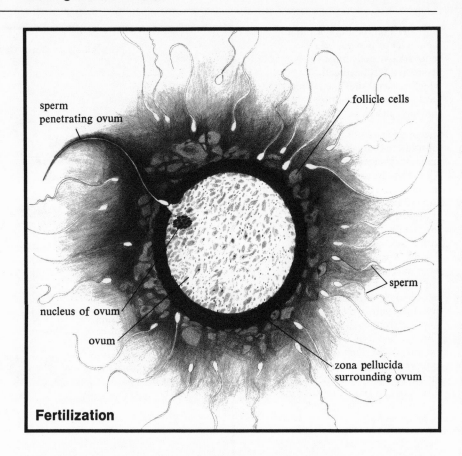

Fertilization

In order to make this possible, special organs of reproduction evolved, along with special behavior patterns. Thus all living species which reproduce sexually possess reproductive organs as well as a strong sex drive and are also programmed to take care of and protect their young.

Mechanisms of reproduction have undergone many changes and improvements in the course of evolution so that today many different methods of mating and young-rearing exist. These behavior patterns of mating and young-rearing are inherited just like our physical characteristics are. In most species, males and females inherit different but complementary reproductive behavior, as well as different but complementary reproductive organs.

Mating and Rearing Patterns

Among most fish and amphibians, fertilization occurs outside of the parents' bodies. The female fish lays eggs, and the male fish deposits his sperm over them. The male or the female of some species of fish are genetically programmed to guard their young before they hatch or even afterwards, while they are still immature, but other species swim away and go about their business after mating. This, of course, is a hazardous process because the eggs could be eaten by a predator or the sperm could be carried away by a wave.

Birds do somewhat better. Birds have a variety of courtship behavior patterns, some of which are quite fascinating. For example, some male birds build "bowers," which are little courtyards that contain pretty pebbles and sticks which the male has gathered and arranged in precise patterns to attract the female of that species. Other birds do little dances which seem to be wildly attractive to the opposite gender of the same species. Like humans, female birds retain their eggs within the body cavity. The male deposits his sperm into her body where fertilization takes place. She lets the fertilized cell develop a while until a shell is formed which offers protection to the helpless embryo. Then, however, she makes the "error" of laying her fertilized egg, often into a nest, where again it is subject to all sorts of dangers.

Many birds are programmed to form "pair-bonds." A male and female bird form a close relationship which entails sharing the tasks of building the nest, hatching the eggs, and feeding, protecting, and teaching their young. Their appearance and behavior are different but synchronized for reproductive purposes. Thus, in some species, the female is camouflaged by dull protective colors and programmed to bravely sit on her eggs and not abandon them even if she is attacked. The male, on the other hand, is brightly plumaged to attract the attention of predators. He is programmed to act as a decoy to lure them away from his mate and his young.

Mammals have developed a superior solution for the problem of protecting their vulnerable immature offspring. The egg is contained in the mother's body, the father deposits his sperm into her, and the baby develops inside her body. This provides pretty good safety for the embryo. In human beings this process is called pregnancy or gestation and takes nine months. After the baby is born, it is still extremely helpless and its protection is insured by the mother's strong maternal instinct which women feel towards their babies. An infant's digestive system is too immature to handle foods which nourish adults. In some infra-mammalian species this problem is solved by programming the parents to swallow food, digest it partially, and then regurgitate the predigested food into their babies' mouths. Mammals have evolved a more appealing solution to the problem of nourishing the infant. Female mammals have developed mammary glands or breasts. A few hours after the birth of a baby, the cells of the breast are triggered into milk production. This means that they steal fluids, nourishing substances, and antibodies from the mother's bloodstream, and convert them into a special liquid, milk, which contains all the material the infant needs to survive and grow and be protected from disease, in a form that his immature digestive system can assimilate. A further improvement in child care in some animal species is the family. In such species mother and father form a strong pair-bond and share the tasks of protecting and teaching and nourishing the growing youngster until he can take care of himself. Thus even love and family feelings have a biological basis and make sense from an evolutionary standpoint.

Again, all these different patterns of sexual reproduction have one thing in common: they depend on an intense sexual drive in both parents. In fish the female seems driven by a strong urge to deposit her eggs in special places which vary with the species, while the male fish seems moved by an irresistible desire to ejaculate or deposit his sperm over those eggs, thus fertilizing them. Fish moved by reproductive urges, like salmon for example, will swim incredible distances and overcome astounding obstacles to do their reproductive thing.

In the mammal, of course, fertilization occurs inside the female's body. Again the motivation for reproduction is very intense. The female mammal, when she is in "heat" or fertile, exhibits a strong desire to attract the male, and also emits a certain odor which evokes strong sexual urges in the male, who is engineered so that he is moved by an intense desire to convey his sperm to his mate's eggs, in other words, to have intercourse. Different species are programmed for specific and different courtship, mating, and childrearing patterns. Some, like us, mate all year around; others mate only during special mating seasons. Some have one mate, others couple with many. Some have family patterns that involve father and mother in rearing the young, others depend exclusively on the mother-child bond for the youngsters' survival.

Higher mammals, including ourselves, are moved by the same basic biological drives which cause all animals to mate, give birth, and rear their young. However, human reproduction goes far beyond biology, or the mechanical joining of sperm and egg. Mating and childrearing patterns have evolved to encompass love, intimacy, and caring relationships. These feelings are much more than genital contact between two human beings and are really the most important aspects of the human sexual experience.

Sexual Pleasure

In order to get us to use our genitals and to reproduce, we have been built so that the sexual experience is extremely pleasurable and rewarding for both males and females. The sex organs, along with certain nongenital erogenous zones of the body, are connected by nerves to the "pleasure areas" of the brain. Pleasure is experienced when the "pleasure center" is stimulated. There is also a center for pain. The pain–pleasure principle is the steering mechanism for human behavior. We learn to avoid pain-producing situations, and seek those which give us pleasure. Many things can stimulate our pleasure zones and give us pleasure—good food and success, for example. But the pleasure centers are especially activated when we feel sexual desire, excitement, and orgasm, so that we are "rewarded" by a feeling of pleasure each time we use or even think about using our sexual apparatus. The connection between sex and pleasure contributes to the survival of our species. For it is only those species who are reinforced or rewarded by pleasure when they engage in sex, and who have an intense urge to mate, who survive the evolutionary elimination race. A species has to reproduce to survive, and we would never go through the rather burdensome business of finding a mate, of courtship, or mating, of giving birth, and of rearing the young if sex were not so pleasurable, and if sexual attractions were not so strong. Is it not strange that we have been taught to feel guilty and secretive about sexual pleasure when it is responsible for our very existence!

The Sex Organs

Males and females have different sexual organs which are designed to manufacture germ cells and to bring the male and the female cells together. The sex organs of both genders can be divided into the genital organs and the organs of reproduction. The genitals are external. They include the penis and testicles of the male and the vulva and vagina of the female. These are for sexual intercourse. The reproductive organs are internal and are needed to store and deliver semen in the male and to provide a fertilization site, shelter, and nourishment for the embryo in the female.

Our internal reproductive organs are invisible and "silent." We only know we have them because we are told about them, not by our own experience. But we certainly know our external genitals. We can see them, smell them, and touch them, and feel things with them. In fact, as we have just seen, the penis, clitoris, testicles, and vulva are not only very sensitive to touch, but can also give us intense erotic pleasure when they are stimulated. When they are touched, reflexes are set off which change their shape and prepare them for sexual activity. Our internal reproductive organs, are "silent" like the stomach, the heart, and other internal organs, and we do not feel them when they function. Thus, they are not part of our body image. Though they are supplied with nerves that produce reflexes that change their shapes and functions, they do not have sensory nerves like those in our skin. Sensory nerves are connected to those parts of the brain which perceive information from the external world. They allow us to feel, to recognize things, and they color our experiences as pleasurable or distressing. Thus we are not even aware that we have internal organs unless they give us pain as a warning of disease or injury.

The Male Genitals

The male genitals consist of the penis and the testicles. The penis carries out two important but separate functions: urination and reproduction. It is a marvel of engineering. When it is soft, it serves as a

The Male Genitals

The drawing depicts the genital organs of an un-aroused, circumcised adult male. Just as there are individual differences in facial features, the size and shape of the normal genitals also vary. Pubic hair may be fuller or sparser or curlier. It ranges in color from gray, black, red, brown, to blond just as head hair does. The shaft may be thicker, thinner, longer, or shorter. The testicles hang lower or higher and are covered with more or less pubic hair. The glans penis is the most sensitive part of the male genitals. It contains the urethral opening through which both urine and semen emerge (but not at the same time).

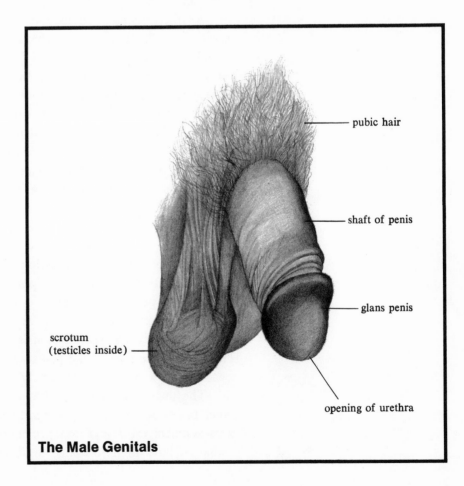

pubic hair

shaft of penis

glans penis

scrotum
(testicles inside)

opening of urethra

The Male Genitals

perfect passageway for urine from the bladder, and when it becomes hard and erect it can penetrate the vagina and deposit sperm where they are likely to find an egg.

The penis consists of a thick tube of tissue which contains within it three smaller tubes all of which are wrapped together inside a tough sheath (the Buck's fascia). The whole organ is covered by sensitive skin which contains special nerve endings which are capable of transmitting exquisite pleasure but only when it is employed for sexual or reproductive purposes. Two of the tubes are called corpora cavernosi (bodies of the caverns) and the third is the corpus spongiosum (body of sponge).

As their name suggests, the two corpora cavernosa are composed of small "caverns" or chamberlike compartments which are capable of holding blood. These little chambers, together with the penis' special blood supply, hold the secret of its dual function. The penis is richly invested with arteries which carry blood into it. These arteries can expand greatly. This expansion is controlled by reflexes. The penis also contains veins, which carry blood away. These can be closed off by special valves. Again, these valves are controlled by reflex action. When the penis is flaccid—that is, limp, the caverns or chambers and also the arteries are relatively empty and collapsed. Then, with the onset of sexual excitement, the arteries expand, and the valves of the veins snap shut. Blood is trapped in the penis and fills the caverns. They expand against Buck's fascia and the penis becomes erect and firm. Thus erection is really produced by a hydraulic system that utilizes blood as the "pumping up" fluid.

The corpus spongiosum is a soft, spongelike structure which cradles the urethra, the tube that conducts both urine and semen. At the tip of the corpus spongiosum is the highly sensitive glans penis. The glans is the part of the penis which is most richly supplied with sensory nerves, making it extremely receptive to stimulation.

The uncircumcised penis has a fold of skin called the foreskin which hangs over the tip of the penis when it is not erect. The foreskin retracts during erection. In our society most baby boys are circumcised —that is, have their foreskin surgically removed—a few days after

The Penis

The penis is composed of three cylindrical masses of spongy tissue. They are held together by tough connective tissue. The three tubes are shown without their covering and have been separated in the upper drawing to show their shape and how they are connected. The two corpora cavernosa are spongy cylinders that end in the soft and sensitive glans penis. The glans provides a cushion at the tip of the penis and protects the female from injury which might occur during vigorous intercourse (the corpora cavernosa are quite hard when they are filled with blood during erection). The lower drawing shows the penis in cross section at midshaft. The corpus spongiosum, which contains the urethra, is shown on the lower part of the penile cylinder. The two corpora cavernosa are shown with their "trabecules" or little caverns, which, again, fill with blood during excitement to produce erection. The connective tissue or fascia and skin wrap up and protect the inner penile structures. These coverings also contain the vessels which supply blood and the nerves which carry messages from and to the genitals. These nerves mediate the sexual reflexes which produce erection and orgasm.

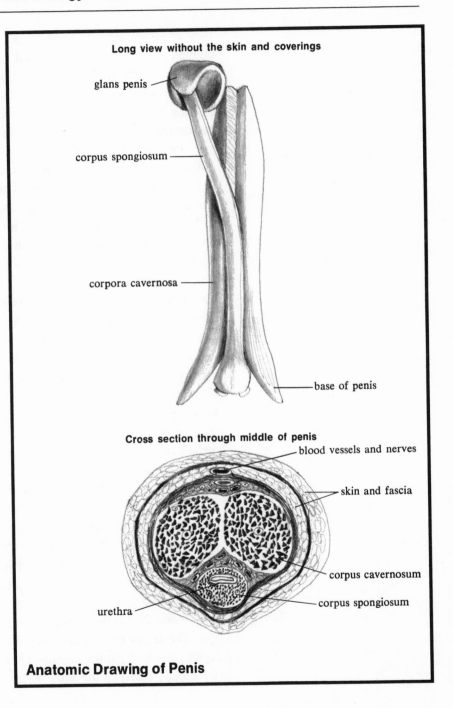

Long view without the skin and coverings

glans penis

corpus spongiosum

corpora cavernosa

base of penis

Cross section through middle of penis

blood vessels and nerves

skin and fascia

corpus cavernosum

corpus spongiosum

urethra

Anatomic Drawing of Penis

they are born. This is done for religious and/or health reasons. Circumcision does not affect sexual functioning, and the sexual experience of circumcised and uncircumcised males and their partners is probably similar if not identical. Sometimes the foreskin is too tight, causing pain and difficulty on erection. This is called phimosis and can easily be corrected by a physician.

Penises vary considerably in size, and the size of one's penis is determined by heredity. Unless a man has a specific hormone problem, which is very rare, there is nothing one can do to change it. Flaccid, the normal penis ranges from 1½ to 4 inches; erect, from 4 to 8 inches, the average being 6 inches. Some men who have a small flaccid penis have a large one on erection. On the other hand, some males whose penis is quite large while flaccid do not exhibit a proportional increase when erect.

For many males the size of their penis is a matter of great concern. This is understandable because we have been taught to believe that the size of a man's penis is a matter of pride. But actually, it makes no sense to worry about the size of your penis because it has no bearing on how much sexual pleasure the man experiences or how desirable he is as a sexual partner. The fact is, men with small penises have as many children and experience orgasms and erections that are just as good and pleasurable as do men with large penises. Nor is the penis size important for many women. A woman's response is usually influenced far more by the man's sensitivity and skill in making love and by his responsibility than by the size of his penis.

The testicles are two sacks of skin near the base of the penis. They consist of the scrotum, a bag of muscles and skin that is covered with pubic hair, and inside the scrotum, the testes, or male sex glands. The testicles have some erotic sensitivity, though they do not respond to being touched as intensely as does the penis. The muscles of the scrotum contract reflexively to draw the testes up when the skin on the thigh is touched, when it is cold, and just prior to orgasm.

The testes are the male sex glands. They are really reproductive organs and not genital organs even though they are located outside of the body cavity in the adult male.

The Internal Male Reproductive Organs

Most males aren't aware of the fact that they have internal reproductive organs. But they do, and they are vital for reproduction. They consist of the testes, where the sperm is produced, plus the various tubes and storage places necessary for the preparation and ejaculation of semen from the penis during sexual intercourse.

The testes are the male sex glands or gonads. They are shaped like eggs and contain two kinds of cells which carry on the two functions: one kind produces sperm and the other manufactures a group of hormones called androgens, which includes the important hormone testosterone, of which more will be said later.

The testes contain numbers of tiny tubules, the seminiferous-tubules. Within these, millions of sperm are constantly produced at a rapid rate. In the healthy male who has a normal hormone level, sperm production continues from puberty until advanced old age. The sperm is also a marvel of engineering and will be described in the chapter on reproduction.

The testes also contain glandular cells which produce androgen. Androgen serves four important functions: 1) in fetal life it causes the embryo to become male. 2) In adult life it is responsible for activating the sex centers in the brain and so gives us sexual desire. 3) It makes the genitals grow to adult size and keeps them functioning, and 4) It causes the development of male and female secondary sexual characteristics in sexually dimorphic species. We are such a species, and that means that human males and females have distinctive characteristics. The male sex hormone, testosterone, and the female sex hormones, estrogen and progesterone, are responsible for creating gender differences. The sex hormones become active during puberty and will be discussed when we reach that topic.

The accessory male reproductive organs serve to transport and store sperm until they are ready to be discharged during orgasm. Sperm travel from the testicles up tubes called the vasa deferentia (sperm ducts), through the inguinal canal into the pelvis. Sperm are stored in the sperm ducts until orgasm. Nearby and connected by the

The Male Genitals and Reproductive Organs

This drawing shows the male genitals and reproductive organs in side view. The testicles and penis, i.e., the genitals, hang down below the trunk. The inner male reproductive organs, which consist of the sperm ducts (vasa deferentia), the seminal vesicles, and the prostate gland, lie within the pelvic cavity. Sperm are manufactured in the testes and travel up into the sperm ducts where they are stored. The sperm ducts empty into the posterior urethra, as does the prostate gland and the seminal vesicles. (The connection between the sperm ducts and the urethra is not shown in this drawing.) When the man ejaculates smooth muscles of the vasa deferentia, seminal vesicles, and prostate gland contract. The sperm is thus propelled into the posterior urethra where it mixes with fluids from the seminal vesicles and the prostate gland. Now it is called semen. The semen then spurts out of the tip of the penis through the penile urethra, via the action of genital muscles near the base of the penis.

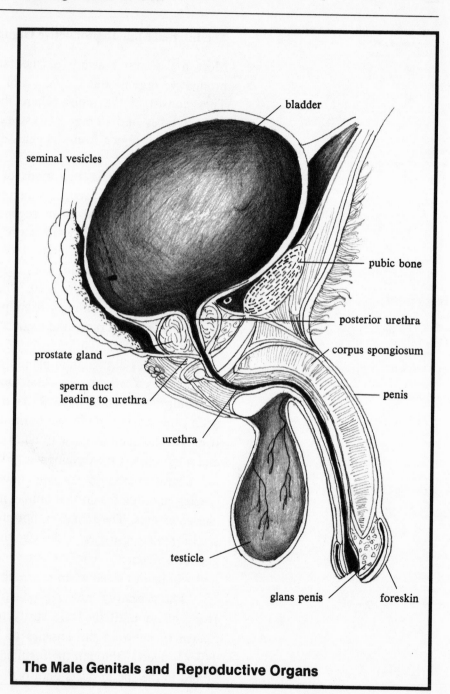

The Male Genitals and Reproductive Organs

The Testes

This schematic drawing of the
testicle shows its inner
structure and its organization.
It contains many yards of
tiny tubes, which constantly
produce millions of sperm
cells on their inner walls. This
is shown in the cross section
of a seminiferous tubule
with maturing sperm cells. The
tubules come together in the
epididymis which forms a
little bump on the top of the
testes inside the scrotal sac.
There the sperm complete
their maturation and become
motile. The tubules then
coalesce to form a single tube,
the vas deferens or sperm
duct. The sperm are stored in
the vas deferens which carries
them into the body cavity
through the inguinal canal in
the groin where it connects
with the penile urethra.
Not shown in this drawing are
the glandular cells located
between the seminiferous
tubules in the testes. These
cells, called Leydig cells,
produce the important male
hormone testosterone.

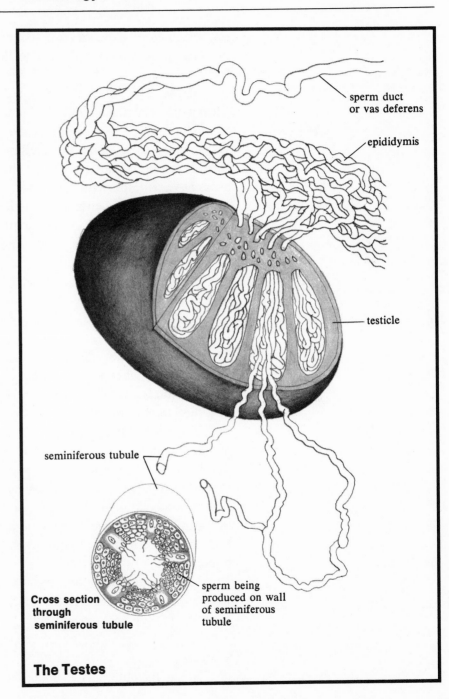

sperm duct
or vas deferens

epididymis

testicle

seminiferous tubule

sperm being
produced on wall
of seminiferous
tubule

Cross section
through
seminiferous tubule

The Testes

tiny ejaculatory duct are two glands, the seminal vesicles and the prostate gland which both secrete fluids that, added to the sperm, forms semen.

Semen is a milky, mucid liquid which spurts out of the penis when a man ejaculates. It has a characteristic slightly pungent odor. It is conducted from the region of the prostate gland and the seminal vesicles in a tube called the urethra down through the penis. This same tube also carries urine through the penis from the bladder, but as we have said, the penis's two functions, urination and reproduction, are kept separate. During ejaculation, a little valve automatically closes the opening between the urethra and the bladder. The engineering which separates urine from semen is so effective that in the healthy male it is impossible for urine to escape through the penis during ejaculation. The same mechanism also makes it difficult for males to urinate while they have a full erection.

The Female Genitals

The female genitals, though not as prominent and visible as the male's, are probably just as sensitive and pleasure-giving. The external female genitals are called vulva. The vulva is composed of the external lips, the internal lips, the clitoris, and the entrance to the vagina.

The clitoris, the small knob of tissue at the front of the vulva, is the seat of female sexual excitement. This organ is the female counterpart to the glans penis and corpus spongiosum of the male. It probably has the same sort of sensitive nerve endings connected to the "pleasure centers" of the brain as does the penis, and its sole function is to transmit sexual pleasure and trigger orgasm. It is partially covered by a fold of skin called the clitoral hood which is analogous to the male foreskin.

Surrounding the clitoris and the vaginal opening are two folds of skin known as the labia (Latin for "lips"). The labia major, or outer "lips," are fleshy and covered with pubic hair, while the labia minor, or inner "lips," are thin and hairless. The labia are erotically sensitive to touch.

Below the clitoris is a small, almost invisible opening connected

The Female Genitals

The shape of the normal female genitals also varies quite a bit; even the pubic hair may be more or less curly and thicker or sparser. The most important erotic organ of the female is the clitoris. As you can see it is covered by the clitoral hood, which is analogous to the male foreskin. The hood is continuous with two thin folds of skin—the labia minora. These swell and blush as they fill with blood during sexual excitement. The vaginal opening is below the small urethral opening through which urine leaves the body. The outer lips or labia majora surround the entire vulva. They too swell during sexual excitement. The anal opening is below the vagina. The entire vulva is very responsive to erotic stimulation, the most sensitive areas being the clitoris and the vaginal entrance.

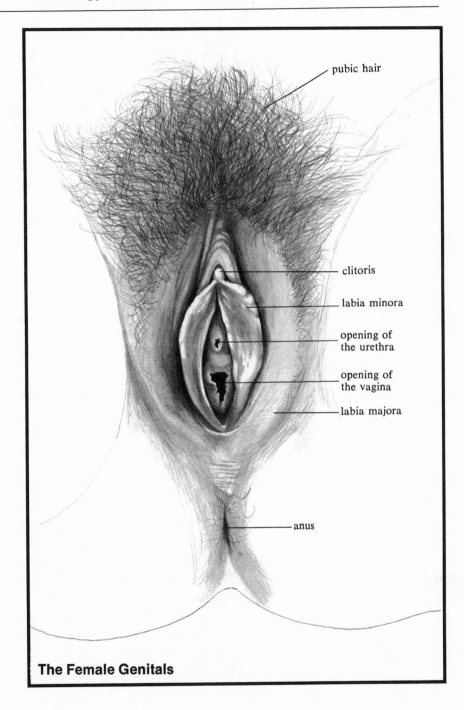

The Female Genitals

to the bladder by the short female urethra. The female urethra, unlike that of the male, has only one function: to conduct urine from the bladder. It has nothing to do with reproduction.

Between the urethra and anus is the entrance to the vagina, guarded by a ring of muscles. The vagina at its entrance is very sensitive. Inside the vaginal entrance is the hymen, a sheet of skinlike tissue which partially closes off the vaginal opening in virgins. Penile penetration ruptures the hymen. It then wears away completely before long. There is a wide range of normal variation in the thickness and blood supply of the hymen. In some cases it is so thin that it is not even noticed at the time of the first intercourse. In other cases it is a little thicker, so that rupturing it produces a slight pain and spills a few drops of blood. Occasionally it is so strong and thick that it must be removed by a surgeon before intercourse is comfortable or even possible.

The vagina itself is a thin, collapsible, elastic tube made of sheets of muscle. Inside, the vagina is lined with smooth, moist cells very much like the inside of the mouth. It provides a passage between the vulva which is open to the external world and the uterus, an internal organ. The vagina is designed to allow the sperm to make connection with the female's egg, which is carried inside her body. The vagina is so elastic that it can stretch to accommodate a baby's head during birth, and then return to its normal shape. Because of this elasticity the normal vagina can accommodate any penis whether it is small or large. It is not too large to provide friction or too small to allow entry. Vaginal flexibility is another reason why penis size is not terribly important in sexual functioning.

The outer one-third of the lining of the vagina is part of the external genitals because it is very sensitive not only to pressure but also to touch. Contact produces reflex changes and also transmits pleasurable erotic sensations. These sensations have a different quality from the sensations felt when the clitoris is stimulated.

The inner two-thirds of the vagina are not sensitive to touch. Therefore, the inner vagina may be considered as part of the internal reproductive organs, although the surrounding pelvic tissues are sensitive to pressure. Thus during intercourse, the female feels the pressure of the penis deep in her pelvis, and also its in and out motions near the sensitive vaginal entrance. The sensation of being penetrated by the erect phallus is considered by many women to be highly enjoyable, and essential to sexual satisfaction. Other equally normal women find less pleasure in penetration. Some actually feel only mild sensations. The clitoris is the most erotically sensitive part of the woman's body, not the vagina. Most women find clitoral stimulation far more erotic than vaginal penetration, but the majority of women enjoy both. Again, even though stimulation of the vagina feels good, orgasm is produced by clitoral stimulation.

The skin and glands located in and around the vulva secrete chemicals called pheromones which have a distinctive odor. This normal genital odor should not be confused with the foul odors caused by lack of cleanliness or infections of the vagina. In many animals the female genital odor acts as an intensely erotic stimulus for the male. Human beings of our culture, however, seem to have mixed feelings about genital odors. Some normal persons find them attractive and other equally normal persons find them somewhat repugnant. Men are often repelled by the female genital odors at first, then learn to accept them, and finally come to enjoy them. It is often the same story with women's attitude toward semen. Most women are repelled by semen at first, but later some learn to accept and even to enjoy its sight, odor, and taste. However, there are some perfectly normal women who do not want to have any contact with semen except in the vagina.

The Internal Female Reproductive Organs

The internal female reproductive organs are all contained in the pelvis, and consist of the ovaries, the uterus, and the fallopian tubes.

The ovaries are the female gonads or sex glands. They develop from the same material that produces the testes and they too have dual functions: the production of eggs or ova, and the secretion of female hormones. The ovaries have many immature egg cells nestling under their surface. Each month one matures and breaks loose from

The Ovary

This drawing of a section through the human ovary depicts the maturation of an ovum throughout one menstrual cycle. Thousands of immature oocytes, which have not even completed their first meiotic division, lie dormant beneath the surface of the ovary. At the beginning of a menstrual cycle, the pituitary gland secretes a follicle stimulating hormone (FSH) which causes several oocytes to complete their first meiotic division and to begin to grow, nourished by the follicle cells which surround them. The follicle cells also produce the hormone estrogen. The oocytes grow within little blisters called follicles, and at some point between the twelfth and fourteenth day of the menstrual cycle, the pituitary sends another hormone, luteinizing hormone (LH), which causes ovulation, or the rupture of the ovum out from the surface of the ovary. After ovulation, the scar, or corpus luteum continues to produce estrogen, but now also begins to manufacture and secrete a second female hormone, progesterone during the second half of the menstrual cycle. If fertilization occurs, the corpus luteum persists and continues to produce progesterone. If the woman does not become pregnant, the cycle begins anew, and the corpus luteum is resorbed into the body in a few weeks.

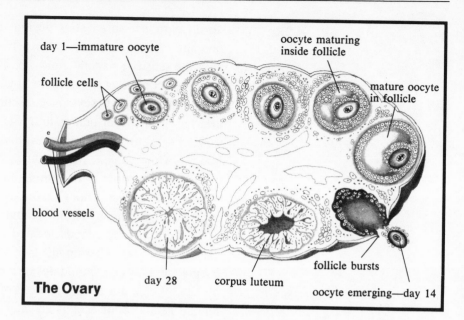

day 1—immature oocyte

oocyte maturing inside follicle

follicle cells

mature oocyte in follicle

e

blood vessels

follicle bursts

The Ovary

day 28

corpus luteum

oocyte emerging—day 14

the ovary and travels down the fallopian tubes to the uterus. The ovaries produce two female hormones, estrogen and progesterone. Estrogen causes the growth and development of the female genitals and reproductive organs. It also produces female secondary sexual characteristics such as breasts and a female hair distribution. Progesterone is the "pregnancy hormone." Both hormones will be discussed in detail later on.

The other female reproductive organs are designed to protect the egg and to provide a favorable place for fertilization and, if it should be fertilized, to shelter and nourish the unborn baby. In its nonpregnant state, the uterus, or womb, is a thick, muscular organ, pear-shaped, about the size of a fist, and lined with layers of cells that are very sensitive to female hormones. It opens into the vagina at the cervix, where the semen is deposited during intercourse.

Breasts. Under the influence of estrogen, the female's breast tissue and nipples grow. Breast growth begins during adolescence when the body manufactures larger amounts of estrogen. We have already mentioned that the breasts are composed of glands which are capable

The Female Reproductive Organs

This diagram shows the shapes and the relationships between the female reproductive organs which have been described. The ovaries are held in place by strong ligaments. As the ovum pops out of the surface of the ovary it is picked up by the octopus-like opening of the fallopian tube. If fertilization occurs, it usually occurs as sperm that have entered the reproductive tract via the vagina encounter the egg as it travels down this tube. The egg continues to travel toward the uterus after fertilization, although by this time it is already rapidly dividing. When it reaches the uterus it implants itself into the thick endometrium or lining, while it waits for the formation of the placenta. The uterus is shown in its small, thick non-pregnant state, but of course, it extends greatly as the baby grows. During labor, the muscles of the uterus contract so strongly, that they push the baby out through the vagina.

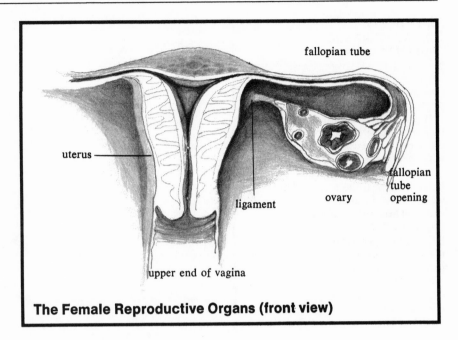

The Female Reproductive Organs (front view)

of taking nutritive material out of the mother's blood stream and out of this, manufacturing milk which a newborn baby with an immature digestive system can absorb. The milk is conducted through little ducts which all converge in the nipple. The baby obtains milk by sucking on the nipple. The sucking reflex is necessary for an infant's survival and is present at birth. A woman's breasts are designed to provide nourishment for the infant. They enlarge during pregnancy and secrete milk right after the baby is born. They will go on producing milk as long as the baby suckles. Milk production is controlled by a hormone secreted by the pituitary gland.

The breasts, and especially the nipples, are also sexual organs in that they arouse the male and give pleasure to the female when they are stimulated. They are erogenous zones—that is, touching them feels good and produces sexual pleasure. Having their nipples stimulated is also arousing for some men.

Normal breasts vary widely in size and shape. Unless there is a hormone problem, which is uncommon, female breast sizes range from

The Female Reproductive and Genital Organs

The labia, the clitoris, and the entrance of the vagina are known collectively as the vulva. Again, these organs are extremely sensitive. The vagina connects the external genitals with the internal reproductive organs. The vaginal barrel ends near the cervix which is the entrance for the sperm. These reproductive organs are "silent." The fallopian tubes arise out of the uterus and open like a funnel near the ovaries where they are ready to catch the egg as it ruptures out of the surface of the ovary during ovulation.

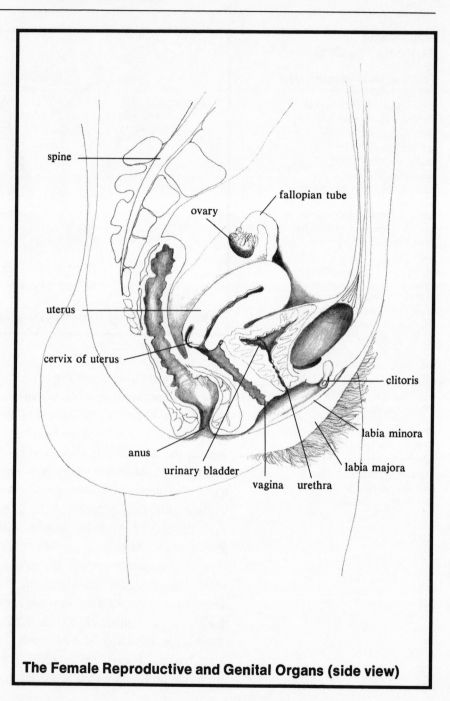

The Female Reproductive and Genital Organs (side view)

The Breast

The breast is made up of glands, fatty tissue lying between the glands, and connective tissue which holds the glands and fat together, giving the breast its shape. The glands are connected to ducts which all come together at the nipple.

The breast is a sexual organ in that it is sensitive to erotic stimulation, and of course, it is also the organ of nourishment which supplies the immature infant with simple food until he can find and digest his own food. The breast glands are very sensitive to sex hormones. Thus, they develop during puberty when the ovaries start to produce large amounts of estrogen, and they turn into highly efficient "milk factories" shortly after the birth of the baby triggers the release of special pituitary hormones.

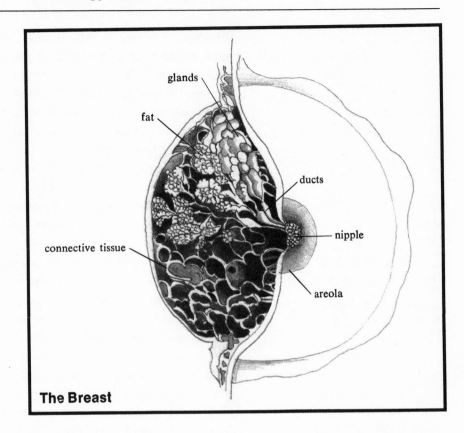

The Breast

A to triple D, and all are physically normal. This is determined by heredity, and there is not much you can do to change them. Different societies and different males define certain sizes and shapes of breast as attractive or as unattractive. In some societies, for example, women with large and even pendulous breasts are much admired, while other societies idealize slim women with small, firm breasts. There is a wide range of opinion in our society as to what shape and size breast is most attractive. Typically in our society the large breasted woman is considered sexy, and large breasted women appear in erotic magazines as the ideal. However, most fashions are designed for women with small breasts, so that it is easier for an A and B cup woman to find attractive clothes than it is for the C and D cupper.

It is not surprising that girls tend to have strong feelings about the size and shape of their breasts. Worry that one's breasts are too small or too large causes many a good deal of misery. Small breasted girls wear padded bras and large breasted girls attempt to hide their bosoms by hunching their shoulders and by wearing baggy clothes. Indeed, some women are so ashamed of their breasts that it interferes with their enjoyment of sex, because they will not let a man see them unclothed or feel their breasts.

A woman's breasts actually are often important to a man's sexual response, but men vary as widely in their preferences as breasts do in their sizes. Some men find tiny breasts more exciting, while others are only aroused by large, full breasts. But a secure person knows that he or she won't be loved by everybody and doesn't worry too much about anatomy: be it height or breast or penis size. It is true some men will not be attracted to you unless you are tall or short, have big or small breasts or slim hips or full buttocks. But a person becomes beautiful and exciting to you no matter what her bra size is if you have a romantic relationship. And if you love him you won't notice the size of his penis. Physical attributes are important; one should try to look good, smell good, and sound good. But appearance can become an obsession, where a minor pimple can ruin your whole day. How you look is important mainly in the beginning of a relationship. Once love is established, appearance becomes relatively unimportant.

Sometimes a girl's breasts develop unevenly, that is, one breast is much larger than the other, or sometimes they really fail to develop at all, or they can grow grotesquely large. Such problems are true abnormalities, and they need not cause a lifetime of misery because they can be corrected by plastic surgery.

Gender

Gender is inherited. One special pair of our chromosomes determine our gender. If you are XX you become female, and if you are XY you become a male. All females have in the nucleii of all of their cells a set of XX chromosomes, while males have XY in every one of

The Male and Female Chromosome Patterns

These photomicrographs of chromosomes were taken from a white blood cell of a normal human male, and a normal human female respectively. The twenty-three chromosome sets have been rearranged in rank order of size to simplify inspection. Notice all the chromosomes are alike for the male and the female except the XX and XY pairs. The female contains a pair of Xs, one from the mother and one from the father, while the male has one X from the mother's ovum and one Y which it received from the father's sperm. The XY chromosome pattern contains the recipe for the secretion of testosterone early on in fetal development. This suppresses the female pattern which is inherent in all mammalian embryos and so a male individual is produced.

Male   XY   Female   XX

The Male and the Female Chromosome Pattern

their cells. Since germ cells contain only half a set of chromosomes, one half of each man's sperm contain an X chromosome, while the other half contain a Y. All ova contain only X of course, since all the mother's cells are XX. Therefore if a Y sperm fertilizes an ovum a boy results, while fertilization by an X-carrying sperm produces a girl. Thus it is always father's sperm which determines the gender of the offspring!

In the adult, the penis and testicles bear little resemblance to the clitoris, labia, and vagina. But the male and female genitals have a common developmental origin and many similarities of structure and functioning. This is because they are made from the same basic material in the embryo. The tissue which will develop into the adult genital organs is the same in all embryos, male and female, but it develops differently if androgen is present or absent. Six weeks after conception embryos with the male XY chromosome pattern begin to secrete androgen, the male sex hormone. If androgen appears at this critical stage, that embryo will differentiate into a male with male genitals. Unless sufficient amounts of androgen appear at the critical time, the embryo will develop into a female with female genitals. All mam-

The Development of the Male and Female Genital Organs

The male and the female genitals have the same beginnings and are homologous with each other. When the fetus is two to three months old (I) the male and female genitals still look the same. By the third or fourth month (II) of pregnancy, male and female genitals have begun to differentiate. By the time the baby is born (III) the male and female genitals look very different. However, despite the differences in form and function, the different genital parts retain the same nerve supply and probably feel similar in males and females. For example, clitoris and glans penis (a) are homologous and are very sensitive. The scrotum and the labia (b) are also homologous and have much less sensitivity. The primitive genital groove which both males and females still have in the first trimester (c) closes in the male and can still be seen in the little groove that is located between the two sides of the scrotum and on the underside of the penis. In the female the genital cleft does *not* close but becomes the adult groove or opening of the vulva.

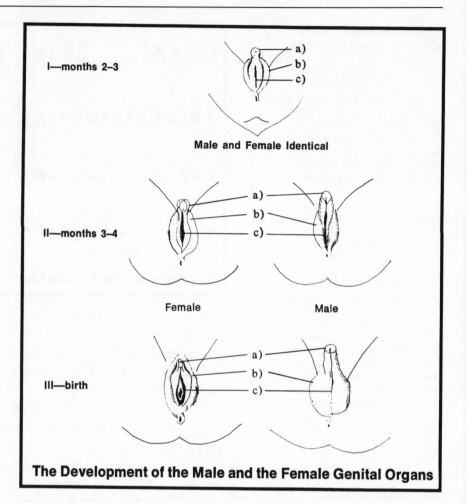

The Development of the Male and the Female Genital Organs

malian embryos would become female unless androgen is added during early fetal life. For example, the little knob of tissue that would otherwise become the clitoris enlarges and becomes the penis when androgen is present. Similarly, the tissue that forms the labia turns into the scrotal sac which later comes to contain the testes. The muscles which would surround the vaginal entrance draw around the base of the penis in the male. These muscles contract during orgasm in the male and also contract during orgasm in the female.

While the external reproductive organs arise from the same tissue,

The Development of the Male and Female Reproductive Organs

The original tissue from which the male and the female reproductive organs will develop is present in all fetuses, those carrying the XX pattern as well as XY ones. Thus, in I, during the first two months of gestation the tissue which will develop into the adult male and female reproductive organs are the same. (a) are the primitive gonads which will develop into the ovary in the female and the testes in the male. (c) is called the Mullerian duct. It develops into the uterus and fallopian tubes of the female. In the presence of fetal androgen the Mullerian material degenerates except for a little remnant. (b) is called the Wolffian duct. In male embryos, the Wolffian material, which deteriorates in the female due to the low amount of androgen, develops into the tubes which store and carry semen from the testicles to the penis, the vasa deferentia (sperm ducts), and the seminal vesicles.

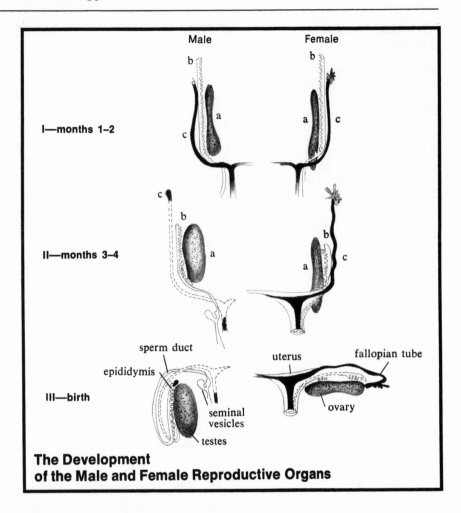

The Development of the Male and Female Reproductive Organs

the internal reproductive organs develop from two kinds of basic material. Both are originally present in all embryos. These "anlagen" are called the Wolffian and the Mullerian material. In the absence of androgen, the Wolffian apparatus disappears and the Mullerian tissue develops into the uterus, the fallopian tubes, and the upper vagina. In the presence of androgen, it is the Mullerian tissue that disappears while the Wolffian material develops into the prostate gland, the seminal vesicles, and the vasa deferentia ducts which comprise the internal male reproductive organs.

The Descent of the Testes

Figure I shows the position of the testes (a), the scrotum (b), and the body cavity (c) during fetal development. A little while before the baby is born, the testes (a) have descended through the inguinal canal in the groin, into the scrotal sac (b). The mature position of the testes is shown in figure II.

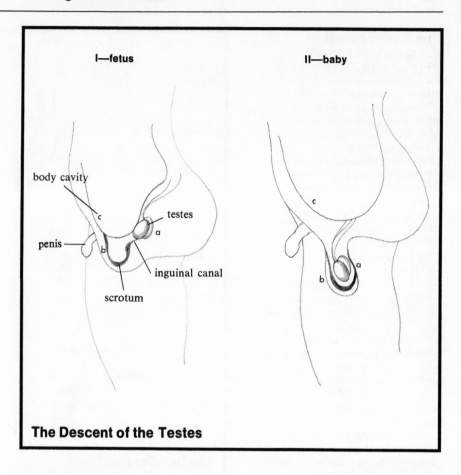

The Descent of the Testes

The testes and the ovaries also arise from the same original primitive material. Under the influence of androgen this tissue turns into testes in the male. The female, who has little androgen, develops ovaries. The ovaries remain in the body cavity. The testes grow at first inside the abdominal cavity, in the same location as the ovaries, but shortly before birth they descend through the inguinal canals into the scrotal sac. If they remain inside the body they won't function normally, probably because the temperature is too high there. It is not unusual that one or both testes fail to descend. If this should occur medical or surgical treatment should be sought to bring them down to insure their proper health and functioning.

The Biology of Sex

Human Reproduction

This diagram puts the pieces together and illustrates the entire process of reproduction. The erect penis is depicted inside the dilated vagina just after orgasm has occurred. Millions of sperm have traveled from the testes through the sperm ducts (vasa deferentia) and have been deposited near the entrance of the uterus. The sperm have traveled into the uterus and through the fallopian tubes where they meet an ovum which one sperm penetrates and fertilizes. The ovum has recently erupted from the surface of the ovary, and after fertilization continues to travel down into the uterus where it implants itself and begins to divide and develop into a baby.

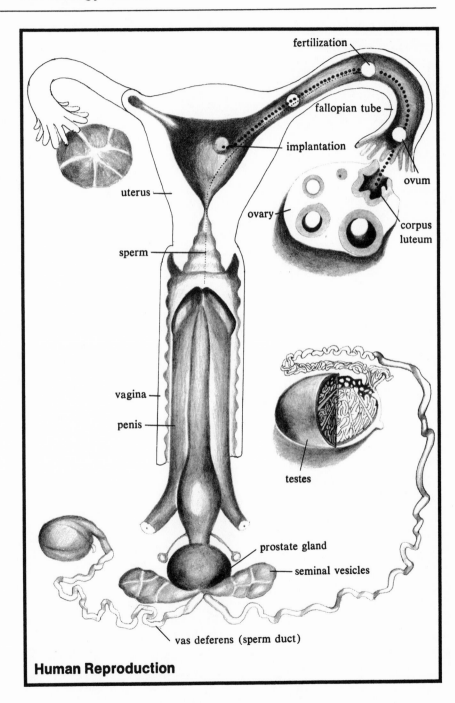

Human Reproduction

THE SEXUAL RESPONSE

Desire, Excitement, and Orgasm

The two people in the lovemaking scene in the beginning of the book first felt desire. Then they fondled each other and became excited—he got an erection and she lubricated. They continued to stimulate each other and both ended with an orgasm. At first glance the sexual experience looks and feels like one smooth sequence, beginning with lust and ending in a climax, but for both males and females it is really made up of three distinct phases: desire, excitement, and orgasm. Now let us examine these phases more closely.

Sexual Desire

Erotic desire, popularly known as feeling "horny," is the wish or appetite for sex. Sometimes you spontaneously feel sexy and are moved to seek out a sexual experience; sometimes, even when you are not particularly interested in sex, an attractive person or particular situation can whet your sexual appetite.

All appetites—hunger, thirst, fatigue, that is, the urge to sleep—

as well as the desire for sex originate in the brain. The sexual appetite arises in a special part of the brain which is located in the area which controls emotion. It is composed of complicated neural circuits and centers, and when these are activated, one feels "horny." The sex centers and circuits in the brain are relatively inactive during childhood. At puberty, androgen production increases in both males and females. This influx of androgen activates the brain's sex centers and this is how we become capable of experiencing sexual desire.

Physical as well as psychological forces can affect the sexual centers and a person's sexual desire. If you are ill, or depressed or anxious, or up or down on certain drugs, or if you have gotten the message that sex is wrong, or if you have been hurt or rejected, you are not likely to feel much sexual desire. On the other hand, if you are in good physical condition, if your mood is good, if you feel that sex is O.K. and especially if you are in love or with someone whom you find attractive, you are likely to feel very sexy. The next chapter on sexual problems deals in greater detail with what can turn your sexual desire "off" and "on."

Sexual desire is felt by women as well as men, but in our society, at least, the experience is not always the same for both genders. Young males, for one, seem to have a stronger sex drive than young females. But this changes as they grow older. During middle age, women who have had pleasurable sexual experiences catch up and sometimes even surpass men in their desire for sex. There also seem to be some differences between males and females in how the relationship with the partner affects a person's sexual desire. Both men and women are more likely to desire and enjoy sex with a partner they love than with a stranger, but men do seem, on the average, to find it easier to enjoy sex with an unknown partner. Physical attractiveness is often more important to males than to females. But this is only a relative difference, as many girls are "turned on" by an attractive male.

Love is a sexual stimulus for both males and females. The state of being in love intensifies one's sexual desires and responses. If a casual friend of the opposite sex touches you, you are probably not going to have a sexual response, whereas all the person you are in love with, or have a "crush" on, has to do is brush your hand, even by accident, and you may become sexually aroused. This link between love and desire is so close for some women that they find it impossible to desire or respond sexually to anyone unless they love him. There are many equally normal men for whom this is also the case, but, in our society, they are outnumbered by the women.

Sexual Reflexes

The second and third phases of the sexual response, excitement and orgasm, differ from desire in that they are marked by physical changes in the genital organs. These reactions which prepare the genitals for their reproductive functions are produced by a series of automatic reflexes. These have already been mentioned, but to make sense of the sexual response, the concept of reflexes has to be explained.

The body is controlled by a whole series of reflexes which adjust it to changes in the outside world and in its inner state. For example, if a foreign body flies into your eye, your eyelids automatically shut tight. This action, produced by a reflex, protects the eye against injury. There are all kinds of reflexes in the body, some protect us, balance us, coordinate our movements, drive our hearts, and keep us from starving. Reflexes control muscles, glands, and blood vessels, which are all under the control of nerves.

Reflexes depend on connections of a sensory organ to a motor organ by a chain of at least two nerves. For example, there is a pain receptor in the cornea of the eye. This is connected to a sensory nerve. This sensory nerve runs into the central nervous system where it connects with a motor nerve. The motor nerve runs out of the central nervous system to an eyelid muscle. When dust hits the cornea it stimulates the pain receptor. This stimulates the sensory nerve which in turn stimulates the motor nerve which then causes the eyelid muscle to contract.

In actual fact sensory nerves usually do not connect directly to

The Eye-Blink Reflex

This diagram illustrates the basic reflex arc. The basic elements of a reflex arc consist of a sensory end organ, a sensory nerve, a connecting nerve, a motor nerve, and a motor organ. The eye-blink reflex protects the delicate eye from injury. When a foreign body flies into the eye, a sensory nerve ending in the cornea is stimulated. It sends impulses via a sensory nerve to the central nervous system (CNS) where it connects with an internuncial or connecting neuron. The connecting neuron stimulates the motor nerve which is connected to and controls the end organ which in this case is the muscle which closes the eyelid. Nerve impulses travel so fast that the eyelid snaps shut a fraction of a second after a piece of dust flies into the eye. This stimulus-response sequence governs many bodily functions including our sexual responses. This again suggests that sex is a *natural biological function* just like many others that enable us to live and thrive in our complex environment.

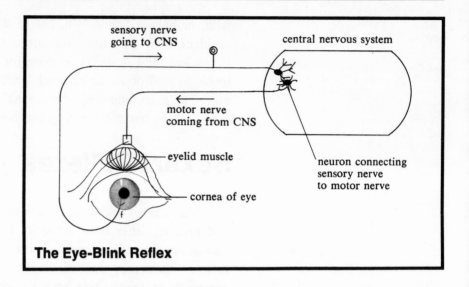

The Eye-Blink Reflex

motor nerves, but are connected to each other indirectly through a number of connecting nerves. Such a tangle of connecting nerves, which are located all throughout the central nervous system, are called reflex centers. In the male there are two erection centers in the spinal cord and a separate orgasm center. Presumably females also have two spinal excitement centers and one which mediates the orgasm reflex.

Reflex centers can be controlled by messages from the higher centers of the brain. This is how your state of mind can make it easier or more difficult to have an orgasm or to get excited.

Reflex changes in organs, to prepare them for specific biological function, are not confined to the genitals. Our bodies are organized so that our inner organs are not perpetually in a state of readiness to perform their special function. That would be wasteful. Most organs just lie there "resting" until reflexes change them to prepare them for action. For example, reflex changes regulate digestion. When not eating, one's stomach is a pale, quiet bag of relaxed muscles. When food is swallowed, however, involuntary reflexes transform the stomach into a churning, writhing organ which is richly engorged with blood, and which by the activation of glandular cells pours out hydrochloric acid and digestive enzymes. The stomach literally turns

The Orgasm Reflex of Males and Females

Orgasm is a reflex which works on the same principle as all other reflexes in the body, e.g., the eye-blink reflex. In the case of orgasm, the sensory end organs are located in the skin of the penis of the male and the clitoris of the female. Sensory impulses travel via sensory fibers of the pudendal nerve to the orgasm reflex center in the spinal cord where they connect to connecting neurons. The connecting neuron stimulates a motor nerve which triggers the genital muscles that produce orgasm. These muscles, which are homologous in the male and the female, are located at the base of the penis in males, and surround the vagina in the female.

The orgasm reflex center in the spinal cord is also influenced by the brain. The brain contains both pleasure and pain areas which are connected to the genital reflex centers. In this way your psychological state can facilitate and enhance your orgastic experience if you are free sexually. But if you are in conflict, for some reason one part of you doesn't want to have sex, your brain can block or spoil the pleasure of your orgasm response. This block is not under your control. Notice, that although the male and the female sexual response seems so different, it has many basic similarities.

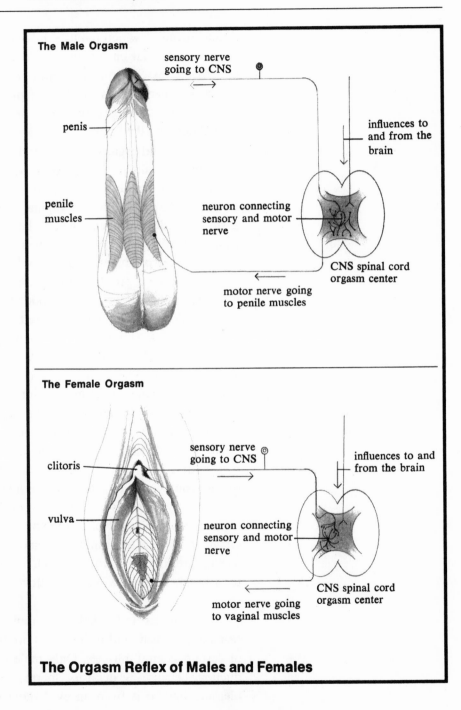

The Orgasm Reflex of Males and Females

into a "blender" which reduces the size of the food particles and mixes them with special chemicals. These changes are produced by vascular (blood vessel), muscular, and chemical reflexes which allow the stomach to perform its function of preparing the swallowed food for its trip down the digestive tract where it is eventually digested and assimilated into the body.

The genital organs of males and females undergo similar changes to prepare them for the job of sexual intercourse. In the male one set of reflexes produces excitement or erection which makes the penetration of the penis into the vagina possible, the other set causes orgasm which deposits sperm where they can do their job of fertilization. In the female, excitement causes vaginal lubrication and swelling, while orgasm produces pleasure only. The excitement phase of the sexual response is produced by genital vasocongestion in both genders. Essentially this means that the blood vessels in the genitals expand and fill with blood. Vasocongestion itself can occur in many parts of the body by reflex action and for many different reasons. When you are embarrassed, it may occur in the skin of your face, for example, and you blush. When you are aroused it occurs in your genitals and if you are a man, you get an erection; if you are a woman, the tissues of your vulva swell and your vagina lubricates.

For both men and women, genital vasocongestion is brought about through the action of the autonomic nervous system. This means that they are not under one's voluntary control. In other words, you cannot directly *will* the lubrication of your vagina or the erection of your penis as you do the raising of your arm. The arm and leg are under the control of the voluntary nervous system. Sexual excitement comes after stimulation, and only if you are relaxed and open to pleasure. In fact, if you try too hard to bring it about, it is not liable to happen, because voluntary effort can inhibit an involuntary response.

Both males and females experience the third phase of the sexual response, orgasm, and in both it is produced by the reflex contraction of certain genital muscles. Only male orgasm is necessary for reproduction because it deposits sperm; female orgasm produces only pleasure and so is from an evolutionary standpoint a luxury. There are significant differences and similarities in the male and the female sexual response and in order to make things clear, the details of the male and the female response will be discussed separately.

The Sexual Response of the Male

Excitement—Erection

During the quiescent, or non-sexual stage, the penis hangs limp and the testicles are lax and loose. Penetration is clearly not possible in this state. Then some psychological and/or physical stimulus starts a series of automatic reflexes that change the quiet soft penis to a hard, actively aroused state so it can perform its reproductive function.

Among the psychological stimuli that can produce sexual excitement are certain thoughts, sights, smells, sounds, and touches. Becoming engrossed in erotic fantasies, reading sexy stories, or looking at erotic pictures can arouse most men, and so can the sound of a pleasant voice, the sight of an attractive or sensuously moving woman, or a gentle touch on the hand, hair, or face. Even the odor of perfume or freshly washed hair can excite a man in some circumstances. The strongest psychological stimuli are kissing and fondling a woman's breasts, buttocks, and body. It is especially exciting to feel her becoming excited by your caresses.

Physical stimuli, or direct touch of the genitals and other erogenous zones of the body, are the most powerful means of producing arousal. Any kind of physical contact and friction applied to the genitals, such as handling, stroking, kissing, or sucking the penis and nearby areas, are highly arousing. Sometimes just the vibration of riding in a bus can can stimulate an erection. Again, this happens because the sensory nerves of the skin of the penis are connected with the erection reflex centers in the spinal cord which cause the penis to become engorged with blood.

The sexual excitement stage in the male is marked by erection, which is produced by vasocongestion. An involuntary reflex opens the

Changes in the Male Genitals during the Sexual Response

During the sexual response cycle, reflexes cause the blood vessels within the penis to expand. It changes from a limp, relaxed organ to a hard, erect one which can enter the vagina and deposit semen near the mouth of the womb. Diagram I shows the genitals in a relaxed quiescent state. In II excitement is marked by erection and enlargement of the penis. The extreme form of the excitement phase, which is sometimes called the plateau stage, is shown in III. This happens just before orgasm is about to occur. Notice that the penis is erect, the testicles have risen. At this time a clear drop of mucus may appear at the tip. This is not semen, but may contain a few viable sperm which can impregnate a female.

After orgasm the resolution phase occurs, which merely means that the extra blood drains out of the penis and it returns to the flaccid state seen in diagram I.

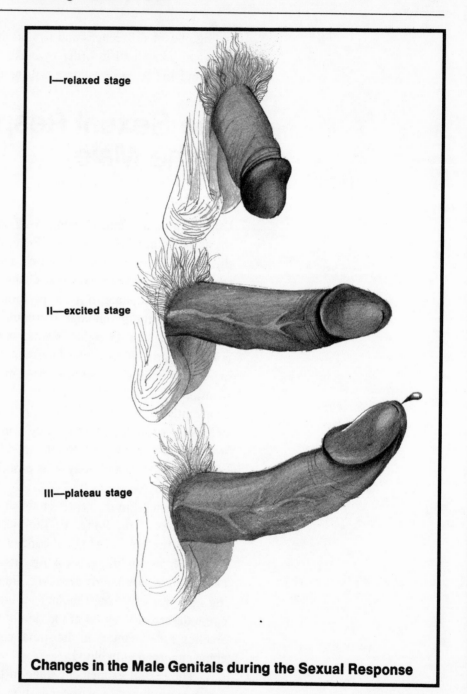

I—relaxed stage

II—excited stage

III—plateau stage

Changes in the Male Genitals during the Sexual Response

penile arteries and closes the penile veins, and the little caverns of the penis become swollen with blood and firm. The evolutionary purpose of the erection is to make the penis hard and erect enough to penetrate the vagina. In those animal species which are equipped with a penis bone (the os-penis), like the whale, erection does not occur because it is not necessary for vaginal penetration.

If the erect penis is further rhythmically stimulated, as in masturbation or intercourse, it reaches an extreme stage of excitement that Masters and Johnson call the plateau stage. This is merely another name for intense sexual arousal. At this stage the penis is fully erect and the testicles rise up close to the base of the penis. If adequate stimulation continues at this stage, the man will reach orgasm.

The Male Orgasm

The reproductive purpose of the male organ is to deposit semen into the vagina so that sperm can fertilize the egg in the woman's body. The orgasm is extremely pleasurable; however, the intensity of the pleasure varies from the mild pleasure of the masturbatory climax to the intense joy of experiencing orgasm with passion.

During orgasm ejaculation occurs, which means seminal fluid emerges from the tip of the penis. It spurts out with considerable force in young men, often having enough momentum to go six inches or more beyond the tip of the penis, but as men grow older the force and distance of their ejaculations diminish. After orgasm there is usually a period during which a man cannot have another orgasm no matter how intensely his penis is stimulated. This period, the time between one ejaculation and the ability to have another, is called the refractory period. The refractory period is shortest when a man is in his late teens through his twenties. At that age he becomes aroused rapidly and with a minimum of stimulation. In fact, some young men are multiorgasmic; that is, they can climax several times in a row and can have many orgasms per day. But sexual responsiveness gradually diminishes, and by the time men are fifty they can usually only have one orgasm at a time, with the refractory period sometimes lasting as long as twelve to twenty-four hours. The normal

frequency of orgasm varies widely from individual to individual. Some
men, some time, feel satisfied after one orgasm, and at other times
wish to have more than one. One should never have more orgasms
than one feels like having. If you try to force yourself, for the sake of
your partner or your ego, if you try to make a performance or an
athletic event of sex, you are heading for trouble. The sex reflexes
may not work if you try to force them and your partner will probably
not admire you for a heroic performance. If she is sensitive she will
feel you are less concerned with her than with an ego trip. On the
other hand, if you spontaneously become aroused again after an
orgasm, and take pleasure in going on, you should by all means
do so. It will not hurt you to have frequent orgasms.

The male orgasm actually consists of two separate phases, each
produced by the contraction of certain genital muscles. The first phase
of the orgasm is relatively "silent" and occurs in the internal reproductive organs. The second phase takes place in the sensitive external
genitals and is intensely pleasurable. As orgasm is about to take place,
the muscles of the inner reproductive organs (the prostate, vas
deferens, and seminal vesicles) contract, squeezing the semen into the
back of the urethra, deep within the root of the penis. This reflex is
called emission. A man experiences a slight sensation at this point,
telling him the orgasm is imminent and cannot be controlled. This has
been called the sensation of orgasmic inevitability and it is followed a
split second later by the pleasurable orgasmic contractions. These
are also reflex contractions but occur in different muscles which are
located at the base of the penis and squeeze the ejaculate through the
urethra and out at the tip of the penis in several spurts at 0.8 second
intervals. After the final contraction, blood slowly drains from the
penis. In ten minutes or so it has returned to its flaccid, quiescent
state.

After orgasm some men feel like resting or sleeping; others are
quite active. It is not true, as some people have believed, that orgasm
drains a man of strength. The testes are capable of producing a vir-
tually unlimited supply of sperm, and expending this supply, even at
a rapid rate, causes no physical harm. For the older man, in fact, sex-

ual capacity continues at a higher level if he engages in regular sexual activity. It is almost literally true that a man "uses it or loses it."

The normal male attains a certain degree of voluntary control over his orgasm reflex. Failure to achieve such control can lead to problems in lovemaking. This topic will be discussed in the next chapter on sexual problems.

The Sexual Response of the Female

Excitement–Lubrication, Swelling

The male's sexual response is more obvious and external than the female's and has, therefore, been understood for a long time. It is only recently that Masters and Johnson devised ways of observing the female sexual response by taking films and electrical recording of the female genitals during excitement and orgasm. We now have some of the data we needed to conceptualize the female sexual response accurately.

Women, like men, can be aroused by psychological as well as physical stimuli. But there are some differences, at least in our society, between what tends to arouse men and what tends to arouse women.

For one thing, women seem less likely to be turned on by visual stimuli than do men. Many men, for example, can become sexually excited by looking at a picture of an attractive nude woman, but fewer women are excited by the image of an attractive nude man. This difference, however, may be disappearing in our society. Certainly physical appearance has always been an important sexual stimulus for both genders. Another difference is that touch forms a more important part of the sexual experience for women than for men. Touching and kissing of the nonerotic areas of their bodies is very arousing for many women. "Foreplay" or the caressing which takes place before intercourse, is usually necessary to arouse the female. This may take a while and may seem tedious to the woman's partner, as men are more rapidly aroused and often do not need foreplay to have a good sexual experience. If a man feels impatient with lengthy foreplay, this does not necessarily mean that the woman is slow or that the man is selfish. It often merely means that he is ready more quickly for penetration, and that their paces have to become synchronized for good lovemaking. Gentle touching of the primary erotic areas, which are the nipples, clitoris, and vaginal entrance, is highly exciting for women but often only after they are already aroused. The most responsive area is the clitoris, which is analogous to the penis. But many women do not enjoy clitoral stimulation unless they are already excited, in fact a direct approach to the clitoris is likely to be a sexual "turn off." Men, on the other hand, generally seem to enjoy direct stimulation of the penis even when they are not already in a state of sexual excitement. Touching a man's penis directly is more likely to turn him "on" than "off."

Excitement in females is also marked by genital vasocongestion. When quiescent, the vagina is a closed, dry, relatively small orifice, but excitement changes it into an open lubricated receptacle which is ready to receive the penis. In the non-aroused state, the walls of the vagina are pale and only slightly moist. Sexual excitement causes blood to flow rapidly into the genital region. As in the male, genital vasocongestion is produced by an autonomic reflex, one over which the woman has no voluntary control. In the excited male the blood is trapped in the penis, causing erection. In the excited female, where there are no caverns or special valves, the blood is distributed more generally around the pelvic areas. This causes the labia to swell and blush a deep red; the tissues around the vagina also swell, forming a thickening inside and around the vagina which has been called the "orgasmic platform." The vagina "balloons" out, in an "internal erection," ready to accommodate the penis. The vulva changes in color from pale pink to deep red and some of the fluid from the blood accumulating there passes through into the vagina. This causes "sweating" on the vaginal walls, and the woman becomes "wet" or lubricated.

Changes in the Female Genitals during the Sexual Response

The female sexual response cycle is similar to that of the male's in that the female genitals also swell up with blood during the excitement phase, because of vascular reflexes. During the excitement phase the vulva and vagina change from their dry, pale, collapsed states and become flushed, swollen, and wet, ready to receive the penis. Figure I shows a section through the vulva, vagina, and uterus during the quiescent stage. More excitement and swelling is shown in figure II. The labia are open and pink, the uterus has risen from its normally horizontal position in the pelvis, and, most important, the vagina is wet and lubricated. III shows the extreme excitement phase, sometimes called the plateau phase. The sexual tissues are so swollen that an "orgasmic platform" or thickening can be felt near the entrance of the vagina. The vulva is bright red. The vagina has ballooned outward and inward, and lubrication is at a maximum. If stimulation is continued at this point, and there are no complications, orgasm will follow.

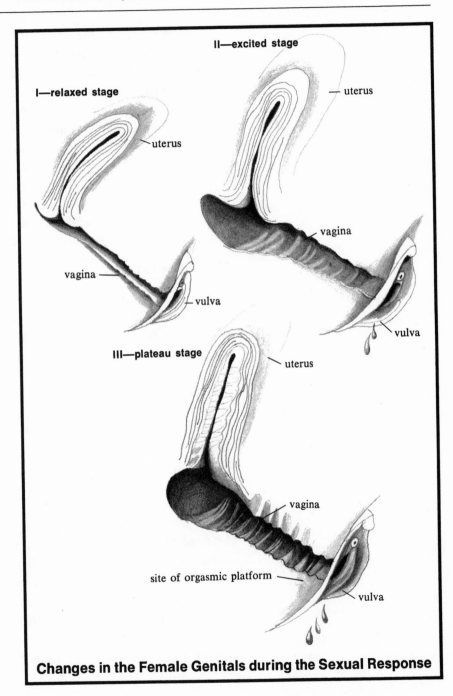

Changes in the Female Genitals during the Sexual Response

Women vary in the amount of lubrication they produce. Some have just enough to lubricate the passage of the penis, while others get very wet. Occasionally excess fluid seeps out of the vagina, which has prompted some people to conclude that women ejaculate some semenlike substance when they climax. Not so. This fluid collects from the vaginal wall during excitement, not orgasm, and it contains no reproductive material like the sperm in semen.

Women do not feel the expansion of the inner part of the vagina during sexual excitement. They are also unaware that their uterus rises within the pelvis when they become aroused. The excitement phase is usually extremely pleasurable for women, possibly even more so than it is for men, who tend to focus more on orgasm.

The Female Orgasm

Orgasm for women is similar to the male orgasm in some respects and different in others. One difference is that while the male orgasm has two phases, the female has only one. The female lacks the first part of the male orgasm, which is emission. Female orgasm consists only of the reflex contraction of the external genital muscles, the same muscles that contract in the second phase of the male orgasm. In women these muscles are located around the vagina and the pleasure of the orgasmic contractions is usually experienced there and deep in the pelvis. The pleasure of orgasm for a woman varies from mildly enjoyable local contractions to the intense psychosexual experience of having an orgasm with someone you love and who loves you.

The male orgasm is triggered off by rhythmic stimulation of the glans and the shaft of the penis, and until recently it was believed that orgasm is brought on by stimulation of the vagina, but we now have evidence that suggests that this is probably not true. Penetration of the vagina is exceedingly pleasurable and gratifying for most women, but orgasm is usually triggered by rhythmic stimulation of the clitoris. And that really makes sense because, as you remember, the clitoris develops from the same embryological tissue as the penis and contains the same kinds of nerves and reflex connections with the central nervous system.

Direct stimulation of the clitoris or the area immediately surrounding it can bring on orgasm without penetration of the vagina. This is what happens in masturbation and in manual or oral sex play with a partner. Of course, orgasm may also occur during intercourse, because then the clitoris is stimulated indirectly: the in and out motion of the penis pulls and rubs the clitoral hood, thus stimulating the clitoris. Also the clitoral area rubs against the man's pubic bone as the couple thrust. This is the way women have orgasms during intercourse. Not all women can experience coital orgasms, even though they may be entirely normal. This is because the clitoral stimulation provided by intercourse or coitus is indirect and not as strong as direct manipulation of the clitoris. This may not be intense enough to produce an orgasm in some women. Many normal women do not reach orgasm during intercourse but can easily respond to direct clitoral stimulation by their partners. It should not cause any concern about the woman's responsiveness, or her partner's abilities as a lover, or the value of the relationship. Couples in which the woman requires some direct clitoral stimulation to reach orgasm can have very

The Way Women Have Orgasms

a: no orgasm at all—approximately 10 percent

b: no orgasm with partner—approximately 10 percent

c: orgasm with intercourse plus clitoral "assistance"—approximately 50 percent

d: orgasm during intercourse without clitoral "assistance"—approximately 30 percent

Women vary in how easily they can reach orgasm. In the past it was believed that all normal women climax on intercourse. But modern experience has shown that in fact only about 30 percent of women can reach orgasm during penetration without any additional stimulation of the clitoris. The above bell-shaped curve depicts an approximate distribution of the manner in which women have orgasms.

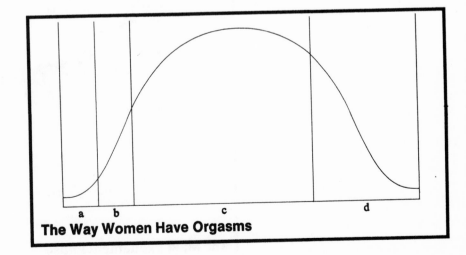

The Way Women Have Orgasms

The Excitement Phase

The excitement phase of the sexual response is produced by the swelling of the genital organs.

In the female the labia swell and "blush," i.e., change from pale pink to bright red or even purple; the vagina becomes lubricated as fluid from the vasocongestion seeps through the vaginal wall; and the uterus rises out of the pelvis.

In the male the caverns of the corpora cavernosa distend with blood and the penis becomes erect; the cremasteric muscles in the scrotal sac contract and pull the testes upward; and sometimes a drop of clear mucus emerges from the tip of the penis.

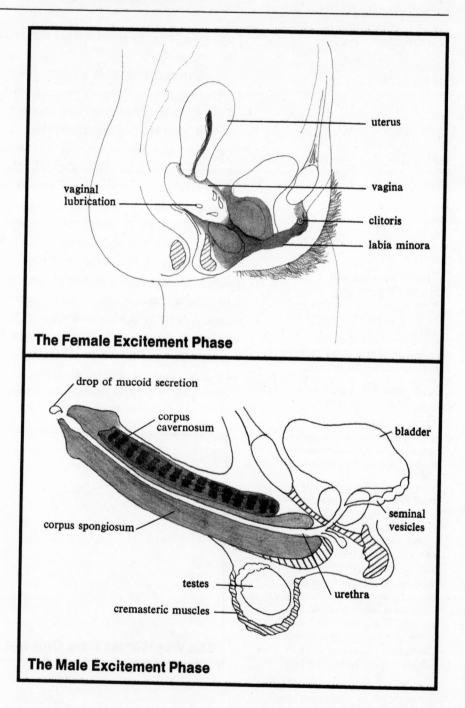

The Female Excitement Phase

The Male Excitement Phase

The Orgasm Phase

Orgasm is produced by the rhythmic contraction of certain genital muscles.

In the female the muscles which surround the entrance of the vagina contract, and this produces the pleasurable sensations of the female orgasm.

The male orgasm has two phases. The first consists of contractions of the smooth muscles of the internal male reproductive organs around the sperm ducts, the prostate gland, and the seminal vesicles. These contractions squeeze the ejaculate into the posterior urethra. A split second later phase II occurs. This is the pleasurable phase of the male orgasm produced by the rhythmic contractions of the muscles which surround the base of the penis. The contractions propel the semen out of the penis. The second phase of the male orgasm thus is analogous to the female orgasm.

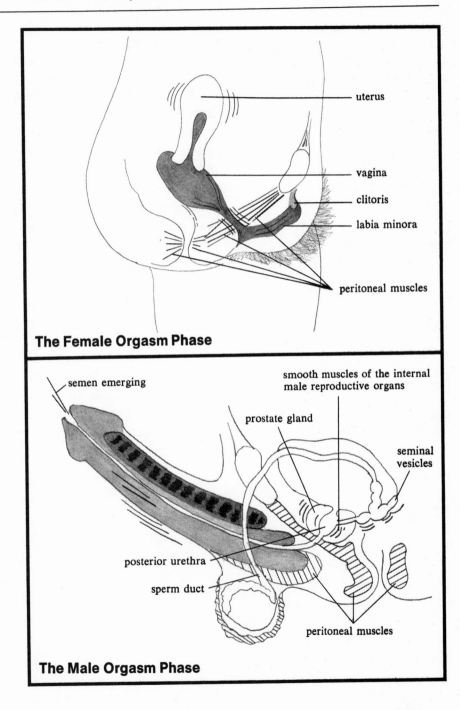

The Female Orgasm Phase

The Male Orgasm Phase

satisfying sexual experiences. However there are some females who find it difficult to have orgasms by any means. This problem can usually be helped and is discussed in the next chapter.

An important difference in male and female sexuality is that women do not have a refractory period of any significant length between orgasms. Even at advanced ages, women can have many orgasms one right after the other. This phenomenon has been called "multiple orgasms." Although they are physically capable of multiple orgasms, however, the desire for them depends on the individual and on the situation; a woman who wants multiple orgasms on one occasion may not on another. Many women are perfectly satisfied and happy with a single orgasm. In fact, the excitement phase of a sex experience may be so pleasurable at times that a woman may not feel the need to have an orgasm at all.

Women are sharply different in this regard from young men, whose orgastic urge is very strong. Young men are apt to be very disappointed if they do not climax after having become aroused. If a male becomes excited repeatedly without climaxing, the resulting vasocongestion may become painful. This syndrome is popularly called "blue balls" and can be cured by having an orgasm. Females have an analogous problem called "chronic pelvic congestion" if they don't climax often enough. This produces a vague, draggy sensation in the pelvic region.

Chapter 4

SEXUAL PROBLEMS
Dysfunctions, Variations, and Gender Disturbances

Sexual problems can be divided into three different kinds: sexual dysfunctions, sexual variations, and gender identity disturbances. The sexual dysfunctions are produced when emotions such as fear or anger diminish sexual desire, or disrupt the genital reflexes that produce excitement and orgasm. In the sexual variations, the genital responses work well and are experienced as pleasurable, but the person's sexual desire is at "variance" with what is considered normal in our society. A person who engages in variant sexual behavior is sometimes called "deviant" or "perverted" because the situations he or she finds attractive are not the ones that excite most other people. Gender identity problems actually have nothing to do with sexual functioning. These problems center around a confusion about whether one is male or female.

The Sexual Dysfunctions

It is impossible to be afraid and enjoy sex at the same time. There are sound biological reasons for this. Fear (or worry or feeling "up tight" or "strung out") is not just a psychological experience. It is an emotion which causes profound physical changes in the body. These changes equip you to meet danger, that is, to fight or to run when something threatens you. For example, when you are frightened a reflex causes adrenalin to flood your body, giving you the quick energy and strength you need to meet danger. Emergency reflexes also shunt your blood away from the organs of digestion and reproduction to supply the large muscles of your arms and legs which are used in running and fighting. These emergency reflexes have absolute priority over anything else, they interfere and overrule all other reflexes including those causing erection and orgasm.

The priority of emergency over sex is useful for survival. Imagine a couple of million years ago making love in the jungle, when a saber-toothed tiger wanders upon the scene. If the couple were to continue their lovemaking they would never live to see another day. Thus animals who survived long enough to produce offspring were those who dropped everything, including eating and mating, and quickly attended to the danger that threatened their very lives.

There may be no saber-toothed tigers around to cause fear today, but there are plenty of psychologically threatening situations which are likely to cause fear and conflict about lovemaking and disrupt sexual functioning.

The priority of fear over sex explains why our sexual responses sometimes fail for emotional reasons. Our sexual reflexes are actually quite delicate, and, since fear is physically the same no matter what its source is, they can be upset by any number of disturbing things. Some of the fears that can ruin an erection or stop an orgasm are rather simple and superficial, such as performance anxiety. The mere thought, "I wonder if I can get an erection tonight?" has kept many a man from functioning that night. Of course other people get frightened when they try to make love for much deeper reasons. Some feel deep guilt about sexual enjoyment, some have gotten negative messages about sex and pleasure from their families, and some have had unhappy childhood experiences that prevent them from the trusting, loving, and letting go which is necessary for good sex.

Some people are very much in touch with their feelings and realize when they are uptight. This puts them at an advantage because when you know you are uncomfortable about something, you can do something to make things better. However there are people who have a way of suppressing and denying unpleasant emotions. Such feelings are hard to face. Therefore they may not even recognize that they are anxious or guilty or in conflict about sex and if you don't recognize a problem you cannot deal with it effectively. It is such unconscious fear and conflict about love, intimacy, and sexual pleasure which is not correctly identified which is responsible for most of the psychogenic kinds of sexual difficulties.

All people probably encounter some problem functioning sexually at some period of their lives because their emotions prevent the sexual reflexes from working right. Emotions can disturb the entire sexual response or can interfere with only one or any combination of its phases: desire, excitement, or orgasm. Thus there are people who feel desire but can't have erections, some who feel little desire but can become erect and have orgasms, some who have intense desire but climax too quickly, and so on. Some of the more common sexual dysfunctions from which people in our society suffer are as follows:

Desire Phase Problems

These are problems in experiencing sexual desire. The healthy person is interested in sex, especially after reaching puberty. It is not normal to be constantly preoccupied with sexual urges, but it is a normal desire which shouldn't be absent for long periods of time. Desire is stronger at some times than at others. It is decreased when one is intensely involved in an activity like sports or studies, and is sharply increased when one has an attractive sexual opportunity, and when with a person one's strongly attracted to.

Desire can be too strong or too weak. It is considered a sickness when a person's sexual desire is so strong that sex becomes a constant obsession or preoccupation. The condition is called "nymphomania" in women and "Don Juanism" in men. Nymphs were Greek goddesses of love and Don Juan was a literary figure whose life centered around seducing innumerable women. Actually an excessive sex drive is so rare as to be a medical curiosity. It is usually a part of some more serious emotional disturbance.

There are persons who are excessively preoccupied with sex or who masturbate compulsively. But most of these do not have a hyperactive sex drive, they are anxious and use sex as a tranquilizer to calm themselves down.

It is much more common for a person's desire to be underactive. Such persons do not feel "horny." Some persons never feel any sexual urges, they don't feel like dating, masturbating, don't have sexual fantasies, and do not become aroused in sexual situations. Others do feel sexual desire when they are alone, but shyness and anxiety interfere with their sexual desire when they are in a romantic situation. Some people only desire a person they can't have, but turn off when they are pursued. Others have unusual patterns of sexual desire. For example, some unfortunate persons don't desire a partner whom they love and respect and who loves them, but are attracted to strangers or inappropriate, cruel, or rejecting persons. This pattern of desire makes for unhappiness and frustration. Sometimes only the desire phase is inhibited. If the other phases are all right, it is possible to respond physically to erotic stimulation with erection or lubrication and orgasm, even if you are not very interested. Like you can eat a meal even if you are not very hungry. However such experiences tend to be mechanical and not really enjoyable.

Excitement Phase Problems

It may happen that a person has a great deal of sexual desire, i.e., feels very horny, but his excitement phase reflexes are ruined by fear. This is more likely to happen to the male, but it is not unheard of in females. As you recall, during sexual excitement, the genital organs fill up with blood and swell. For a man excitement produces erection; for the woman, vaginal lubrication and swelling. Dysfunction in the excitement phase for a man is known as impotence: the inability to achieve or maintain an erection. The term impotence is misleading and a "put down" because it implies the man is generally inadequate. Not so—a man who has erection problems may be adequate and effective in all other areas of life. This is why the term "erection disorders" is preferable. When tense, no matter how desirable the partner or how exciting the situation, some men will not get an erection. Or a man may have an erection during foreplay, but loses it when he and his partner get undressed, or when he tries to enter the vagina, or even when he is in the vagina but before he has an orgasm. Erection problems can be extremely vexing and upsetting because the ability to be virile and potent is an important factor in self-esteem. Actually temporary erection problems are very common and can and do happen to almost every man once in a while. You can understand this if you recall that any kind of anxiety can drain the penis of blood instantly. If you are frightened, the emergency reflexes will cause your blood to rush to your arms and legs so you can fight tigers, not to your penis so you can make love. And everyone, whether he is aware of it or not, has anxiety sometime, especially when one first starts having sex. So usually an episode of erection failure is transient and will not be repeated if you are calm the next time. Therefore you can see that it is very important not to worry about your performance when you make love. Try not to judge yourself. Put everything out of your mind and just "go with" the pleasure. Performance anxiety can escalate into a true and permanent problem if you become too anxious and obsessed about your erections. If you should happen to lose your erection, the best thing to do is to relax and tell your partner how you feel. The erection is not your "last one" and it may return in a little while, or you might feel like postponing sex until the next time. A word of warning about forcing yourself to have sex when you are not in the mood, or if you are not attracted to your partner. *Don't*. Whether you are male or female it is not realistic to expect that you should always be ready for sex with any willing partner. No one is. If you try to go against your feelings, you may have trouble functioning. Another word of warning is about alcohol and other "downers." They interfere with desire and erection on a physical basis. You will function best if you are free of alcohol and drugs. While impotence, especially in young men who are just starting their sexual activity, is often temporary, there are of course men whose erection problem is persistent. For such men treatment is available. The main aim of such therapy is to reduce the man's sexual anxiety so that his excitement reflex just naturally happens.

Women too may be inhibited at the excitement phase and fail to lubricate when they are stimulated. This is analogous to impotence. Usually it is not as embarrassing for a woman to remain dry because it is not as obvious as an erection failure. Women who have sexual difficulties used to be called frigid. This term is as misleading as its male counterpart, impotence. Women who suffer from sexual inhibitions are not necessarily cold or hostile or neurotic. They are merely afraid of sex or not attracted to their partners, or trying to have sex when they really don't feel like it.

Orgasm Phase Problems

No one has voluntary control over desire or excitement. You cannot will yourself to become attracted to someone and you cannot voluntarily erect your penis or lubricate. However most people have some degree of voluntary control over their orgasm reflex. Most people can hurry their climax somewhat or delay it. Orgasm phase problems occur when a person cannot control the orgasm or has too much control so that he or she can't "release" it.

The most common orgasm problem for men is premature ejaculation. In this disorder the man has no voluntary control over his orgasm. He climaxes automatically when he reaches the excitement stage. He may become excited extremely rapidly and climax after one or two thrusts or even before he enters. This shortens the excitement phase and this is most often too quick for satisfying lovemaking. Both the man who comes quickly and his partner may be upset and frustrated by this problem.

Prematurity, when not treated, may be a problem that plagues a man all his life. But this should not be confused with the temporary learning period which many normal males go through when they first begin to have intercourse. Most young men climax rapidly the first few times. It merely takes a little practice before you learn control. Doctors can often teach a premature ejaculator how to control his ejaculations, and some of the principles of treatment can probably help you learn control of rapid orgasm if this is a problem for you.

Psychiatrists used to believe that premature ejaculation was caused by a serious neurosis. Now we have learned that this is not true. Prematurity is a learning problem. It is the men who *do not pay attention to their sexual feelings,* because they are distracted by worry about their performance, overconcern with their partner, or who become anxious when the pleasure of sexual excitement is too intense, who fail to learn control. Therefore, if you want to learn ejaculatory control you should concentrate on your own sexual sensations as your excitement mounts. Focus only on the pleasure you feel in your genitals and "go with" your erotic feelings. If you can do this, you will probably soon learn to recognize "where you are" in terms of arousal. You will learn to enjoy excitement for its own sake, not just as a means of reaching orgasm. You will learn when to slow up and how to "make it last."

The advice to concentrate on your sexual sensations is the exact *opposite* of the "common sense" counsel which is usually offered to "slow a man down." In addition to ointment to anesthetize the penis, and condoms to diminish sensation, men were wrongly advised to think about non-sexual and even unpleasant things like algebra exams. These maneuvers will diminish your pleasure and excitement, but the distractions will actually *interfere* with learning ejaculatory control. If you concentrate on your sexual sensations, you will have more pleasure plus the ejaculatory control you need to become a good lover.

Retarded ejaculation is the opposite kind of difficulty. In this condition the man cannot "let go" and allow his orgasm to happen. Men who have this problem usually feel desire, and have no problems with erections, and yet they have trouble having orgasms even though they receive plenty of stimulation.

Some men are so inhibited that they cannot have an orgasm at all, even in their sleep. Others can masturbate to orgasm when they are alone but the presence of another person inhibits them. When the problem is less severe, a man may be able to climax on manual or oral stimulation by his partner, but not inside the vagina. Some retarded ejaculations merely take a very long time before coming. When this is a permanent problem, a doctor's help is needed. However, it is possible to have an occasional problem with reaching orgasm. If you have this tendency, perhaps the techniques we have found useful in treating patients with this problem might be helpful. The main principle is to *distract yourself* with erotic fantasies while your penis is being stimulated. Distraction is necessary to stop you from "orgasm watching" which is what is probably stopping your ejaculatory reflex. If you recall the way to slow the orgasm is to concentrate on your sensation, and the way to speed it up is to *distract* yourself with sexy thoughts.

Another variation of retarded ejaculation consists of the inability to enjoy orgastic pleasure. This occurs when a man's orgasm consists only of emission, and the pleasurable muscle contractions are inhibited. In this condition semen merely seeps out but does not spurt out of the penis, and the man is cheated out of his orgastic pleasure.

Perhaps the most common sexual complaint of women is that while they have sexual desire, enjoy sex, and lubricate, they have difficulties in reaching orgasm. They achieve a certain level of sexual arousal, but even when they receive plenty of clitoral stimulation, they have trouble climaxing. This problem is analogous to that of the retarded ejaculator, but inhibition of the orgasm phase is much more common in women.

Women vary as to how much stimulation they need to come to orgasm. About 10 percent of adult American females have *never* experienced an orgasm in their lives. Others have learned to have a climax by masturbation when they are alone, but the presence of an "audience," that is their partner, makes them too tense to reach orgasm. Such women fear that they are taking too long or that their lover will reject them if he is required to stimulate them. Some women can reach orgasm when in the presence of a partner, but it takes a long time of intense clitoral stimulation. Some women who take a long time or who can't come "fake it." They pretend to have an orgasm rather than risk the embarrassment of admitting the truth. Some women who simulate could actually climax at a normal pace if they gave themselves a chance, but they are merely oversensitive to rejection and overanxious to please their partner. Faking orgasm interferes with the development of a good sexual relationship, for how can your partner learn to give you pleasure if he doesn't know that you need more time?

Some women can climax during sexual intercourse without direct clitoral stimulation, whereas other equally normal women have a higher orgastic threshold and therefore need direct clitoral stimulation in order to climax. We have already said that both patterns are considered normal by many authorities in the field of human sexuality. But some "coitally inorgastic" women can learn to climax on intercourse with professional help. The principle which helps male retarded ejaculations is also useful for women with orgasm problems. If you have trouble coming, try clitoral stimulation together with distracting yourself from "orgasm watching" by immersing yourself in an erotic fantasy. And if you have never had an orgasm, and feel that you would like to experience this, learning how to give yourself one first before you try to have one with your partner will probably be helpful.

Vaginismus is a female dysfunction that is not associated with a particular phase of the sexual response. Normally during intercourse the ring of muscles surrounding the vaginal entrance relaxes and opens, permitting the penis to enter. In vaginismus the opposite occurs: The muscles go into spasm and snap tightly shut, making it impossible for the penis to enter. Sometimes no cause can be found for vaginismus. In other cases it can be traced to a frightening or painful sexual experience. Vaginismus is essentially a conditioned spasm of the vaginal entrance muscle, that is, it stems from some past learning. But since what can be learned can be unlearned, vaginismus is almost always responsive to medical treatment, which consists of gently dilating the vaginal muscles.

Causes of Dysfunctions

All sexual dysfunctions are not caused by fear. Certain diseases and drugs can cause sexual inadequacy. The most common physical problems of young persons are endocrine (glandular) disorders. Remember that testosterone is needed by both males and females for the proper functioning of the brain's sex centers as well as for the male genitals. Liver disease and mononucleosis can also produce sexual problems. Older persons who have diabetes, neurologic, or circulatory diseases may lose their ability to function sexually. Among the drugs which can ruin your sex life the narcotics (codeine, heroin, methadone, morphine) and alcohol are the worst offenders. Downers will do just that also. Older persons who must take medicine for high blood pressure may suffer from sexual problems as a side effect. Drugs can hurt your sex life, but they seldom help. Although there is a lot of talk about aphrodisiacs, unfortunately no substance which will improve your sexual capability has yet been discovered by medical science. The only thing we know that will enhance your love life is being in love.

Treatment for Dysfunctions

The medically caused sexual problems such as anatomic defects of the genitals or endocrine disorders can often be cured by a physician with proper surgical or medical treatment. But most sexual dysfunctions have psychological causes and these can also often be treated successfully. The main aim of treatment is to reduce the anxiety a person feels about lovemaking so that his sexual reflexes can work properly. And there are multiple causes of sexually disruptive anxiety. Sometimes fear is caused by ignorance and false expectations about sex. In such cases a patient can be helped by providing accurate information about male and female sexuality. It is also important to dispel whatever guilt and fear a person may feel about sexual pleasure. Since such sexual fears and guilt are often beyond the person's conscious awareness, the first step in treatment is to identify this problem and then to raise the person's level of consciousness about his secret fears, wishes, and guilt about sex. Surprisingly, many people, without being aware of it, are afraid of and avoid pleasure and sexual success. When success anxiety is an obstacle to good sexual functioning, professional psychiatric help may be needed to overcome it. Other patients who cannot function sexually are afraid of sexual failure and must be cured of their performance anxieties. Another frequent cause of sexual dysfunction resides in a poor relationship between the partners. It is difficult to have a successful sex life if two people do not understand or like each other. An open and secure relationship where honest communication is possible leads to a tranquil and happy emotional state when you make love, and serves to enhance the pleasure of sex as well as to prevent interpersonal sources of anxiety such as the fear of rejection and ridicule. This provides an atmosphere where both partners can learn to be skillful lovers to each other. The therapist must first evaluate the causes of a couple's sexual anxieties. When these are accurately identified the couple can often be helped by sexual therapy. This consists of a combination of specially structured sexual exercises which are conducted in the privacy of the couple's home. These experiences evoke feelings and reveal problems which are then dealt with through psychotherapy done by the doctor in his office.

"First-Time" Problems

It is very common to be temporarily dysfunctional in the beginning of one's sex life. It has already been mentioned that many young men climax very rapidly the first few times. Also, since the first sexual experience may be especially anxiety provoking, the erection reflexes may not be all that reliable in the beginning. If you remember what the sexual response is all about, that anxiety may temporarily interfere with your sexual desire and with your capacities, that you are human, with understandable anxieties, and that your partner is a human being too, you will probably manage to overcome the difficulties of learning to be a sexual partner rather quickly, without collecting damaging doubts and insecurities.

The fact is that almost everyone worries in the beginning because very few of us are all that secure: "Will she like me?" "Will I have an erection?" "Will I come too fast?" "Are my breasts too small?" "Are they too large?" "Do I have bad breath?" "Will he ask me out again?" "Will I get pregnant?" "Should I be doing this?" "Will he/she know I am a virgin?" "How come I don't feel much?" These are the kinds of doubts which bedevil most of us until we have had some good sexual experiences.

So far we have been concentrating on the "first time" troubles of men, but women face pretty much the same problems when they begin sexual activity. Women get stage fright too, and temporarily lose their sexual desire and fail to become excited. They worry about their performance the same way males do. To compound this problem, many women are embarrassed about letting their partners know about their need for clitoral stimulation because they want to appear to be super-responsive and make the man feel that he is a super-lover. And in addition, women also have to deal with the special problem which arises because penetration is often disappointing at first. The pre-coital parts of lovemaking, touching, kissing, and clitoral stimulation are usually highly enjoyable and stimulating and may be actually the best parts of a woman's sexual experience. If that is good, she thinks, then the "real thing," which to many people means vaginal penetration, must be even more wonderful! Certainly most males love the feeling of vaginal penetration. Well for some women it is wonderful, even the first time. But for many normal females, the first few penetrations are disappointing. A woman may feel very little or she may even feel uncomfortable at first. One reason may be that the woman is frightened and troubled by conflicting feelings about being penetrated. No one can enjoy sex under such conditions. (You should *not* have intercourse unless you truly want to and have resolved any conflicts you might have about this.) Another frequent cause of disappointment is not enough stimulation beforehand. A couple may kiss and caress each other for hours when they do not intend to have intercourse, and then on the night they have appointed for their first intercourse they may skip or hasten through the necessary foreplay and proceed to insertion before the woman is ready. Since he is probably very excited, he may have his orgasm in a few moments, while she has had little pleasure.

The facts of female sexual physiology account for still other cases of disappointment. Again the seat of a woman's sexual arousal is the clitoris. The vagina also has erotic sensitivity, but some women's vaginas only become sensitive gradually and many women only enjoy intercourse after many good sexual experiences. A woman who does not understand that it can be normal to experience little or even no initial sensation in the vagina may conclude that there is something wrong with her. Her discouragement may then prevent the development of good feelings. If intercourse is not especially good the first few times, do not worry, it should get better with practice if you relax.

A myth exists which warns that initial intercourse will be painful for a virgin. In most cases this is *not true*. Some women do experience a slight discomfort as the hymen is ruptured. But there should be no real pain. If it hurts more than a little bit, you are either very tense or there is something wrong medically, and you should see your doctor. If you feel little pleasure or even mild discomfort on penetration the first few times, do not be alarmed. This is a normal and common experience. You should be honest with your partner if intercourse is unpleasant or painful. It does not mean that you are sick or strange; it does not mean that you are a complainer; it does not mean that he is a poor lover. What it does mean is that your relationship with your partner is sound enough and close enough and trusting enough so that you can risk being truly honest with each other.

Apart from being well informed, feeling good about yourself, and being at least relatively free of conflict, one of the best psychological insurances against experiencing anxiety during lovemaking, especially in the beginning, is to avoid lovemaking until you find someone to whom you are close and whom you can trust. In such a relationship, even if all the reflexes work right, if it doesn't feel all that great, it won't be a total disaster. Your partner will not reject you; he or she won't be insulted. You can learn together, and you can become even closer and more intimate if you can share your successes as well as your human anxieties and failures.

The Sexual Variations

The variations are really problems of desire, not in the intensity of desire but in who or what is desired. Most people desire and are sexually attracted by members of the opposite sex and want to have sexual intercourse with some opposite-sexed person. Even sexual fantasies, from an early age on, involve genital contact with persons of the opposite sex. There are some people, however, who do *not* desire sexual intercourse with the opposite gender. They may, however, be attracted to the unusual, to persons of the same sex, to young children, animals, or even to inanimate objects such as shoes or underwear. Some desire unusual activities such as being tied up, inflicting or receiving pain, or exhibiting one's genitals in public.

The most common form of variant sexual behavior is homosexuality. Homosexuals may be male or female. They may behave and move and dress in an entirely normal fashion or they may act in an effeminate manner (if males) or a masculine manner (if females). They may not have any other psychological difficulties and function well at work and socially, or they may suffer from a variety of psychiatric disorders, just like heterosexuals.

A homosexual may have absolutely no desire for members of the opposite gender, but others feel attracted to both males and females. Such a sexual preference is called bisexuality. Most psychiatrists feel that bisexuality is really a milder form of homosexuality.

Psychiatrists are not sure what causes homosexuality. Some male homosexuality may be the result of an insufficient supply of the male hormone androgen before birth. It is possible that too low a level of androgen at this stage prevents the fetal brain from achieving its full masculine potential. However, most authorities believe that homosexuality usually results from a disturbed emotional relationship between child and parents. This disturbed emotional relationship, they think, leads to fear and inhibition of sexual desire for members of the opposite sex.

Many people are falsely afraid that they are homosexual. Most normal heterosexual persons have some homosexual experiences, especially when they are young, and they may find them enjoyable or frightening or both. It definitely does *not* mean you are homosexual if you have tried mutual masturbation or other forms of stimulation with a friend even a few times and even if it felt good. This is a common experience as we have learned from the histories of most normal adult heterosexuals. Other youngsters fear that they may be homosexual when they do not enjoy, or function successfully, in their first heterosexual attempts. Most likely this is the result of worry and anxiety, *not* of latent homosexual tendencies. Strong and loving friendships with members of your own gender also is *not* a symptom of homosexuality.

If you have strong homosexual tendencies, your sexual fantasies will probably be predominantly homosexual and not heterosexual; and you will not be attracted to members of the opposite gender. You will, however, be attracted primarily to members of your own gender.

Some homosexuals are content with their sexual orientation. Others are deeply distressed; they wish to change and become heterosexual. Those who wish to change can often be helped to do so with psychiatric treatment. Treatment for homosexuality is most successful when it is started at an early age, before the sexual preference is firmly established.

The one thing that persons with variant sexual appetites have in common is that they have little or no desire for appropriate sexual partners. They don't *want* to make it with members of the opposite sex of appropriate age in an appropriate way. The infinite variety of things, objects, and activities which can "turn" some people "on" is truly astonishing. Therefore the list of sexual variations is quite long. The most common ones are pederasty (attraction to children), sadism (being aroused by inflicting pain), masochism (being aroused by enduring pain or humiliation), exhibitionism (being aroused by exposing one's genitals), voyeurism (being aroused by watching someone else's sexual activity or an undressed person) fetishism (desiring an inanimate object such as a shoe, or leather, or rubber, or a piece of underwear), necrophilia (desiring a dead person), and being aroused by raping a helpless victim.

The sexual variations described above become problems mainly if they harm others, such as the case with rape or the desire for sex with a small child. Variations also are disadvantageous if the urges are so strong that they prevent the person from other more rewarding kinds of sexual and love experiences. Actually, unusual sexual desires that are mild enough so they can be satisfied by fantasies are experienced by many normal persons and are entirely harmless. This raises the question of what is normal sex? This topic is considered in the next chapter.

While persons who are interested in variant sexual behavior are often not really crazy or out of control, some may be mentally ill and dangerous. Therefore it is best to avoid any adult who behaves in a peculiar manner. If you do happen to be exposed to such behavior you may find the experience upsetting, arousing, or both. These reactions are perfectly normal, but it might be helpful to discuss the experience with someone you trust.

Gender Identity Problems

By the time children are eighteen months of age they have a firm, unalterable, lifelong concept of whether they are male or female. Their gender identity is shaped by the way they are treated, probably from the "messages"—that is, the nonverbal communications—they receive from their family. It is important for the psychological well-being of growing children that they be clearly considered as male or female. If there is conflict in the way children are perceived and treated by the family, they may grow up confused about their gender identity— and be very unhappy with the situation. As adults they may hate their gender so much that they often seek "sexual reassignment." They change their names, their life style, their clothing, and their way of talking and moving to that of the opposite gender. Some even undergo surgical procedures and hormonal treatment to change their physical characteristics. Such individuals are called transsexuals.

Transsexuals are often confused with transvestites. Transvestites are not unhappy with their gender. They merely become sexually aroused by donning the clothes of the opposite sex. That is a kind of fetish.

Gender Roles

Gender roles should not be confused with gender identity. Gender identity is the inner feeling that one is male or female. Gender roles, on the other hand, prescribe how a male or female "should" behave —that is, what roles a male or a female is expected to play in the family and in society.

There are biological differences in the bodies and probably also in the behavior and temperament of human males and females. For example, young males are, as a group, more energetic than young females. We do not yet know the extent to which male and female brains, emotions, and thinking patterns are physically different. However, gender roles are based only in part on the biological differences between men and women—on the fact, for example, that women bear and suckle children, while men are stronger and speedier and better suited to hunt and to protect their families from predators. Most gender role differences have nothing to do with biology. They are a product of tradition and of social and economic conditions. The gender roles practiced in different societies vary widely. Some societies for example practice polygamy while in others polyandry is the prevailing custom. Gender roles also change from one historical period to another, and in fact we are currently in a transition period from a male dominated society to one in which a more equal role of the sexes seems to be emerging. Our traditional gender roles were not entirely without merit. They defined predictable roles which both men and women clearly understood and for which they were trained, both in their responsibilities and privileges. In other words, boys knew all along they were expected to provide for the family, while girls expected to take responsibility for the home and children in exchange for support and protection. But the disadvantages of the rigid role definitions seem to many to far outweigh these advantages.

Some roles assigned to men and women in our society have probably been disadvantageous to both. For example, a "real he-man" was supposed to be tough, strong, and competitive. He was not supposed to show any tender feelings or vulnerability, or to admit that he had a need to be cared for. A "real feminine" woman, on the other hand, was not supposed to compete, or to be interested in achievement, or assert herself. Instead, she was trained to please and submit to the man, who would in turn protect her. But such rigid role definitions ignored individual differences and artificially limited the human potential. Normal men feel good when they can be tender and open without feeling like "sissies" and many normal and creative women enjoy the new freedom to achieve and be independent. In sexual behavior too, old-fashioned gender roles tended to create an artificial situation which often spoiled both partners' pleasure. The man was supposed to always be the "strong one," to perform, to have an instant and perpetual erection, and to take full responsibility for the initiation and conduct of lovemaking, while the woman was supposed to be passive, submit, to please and not to think of her own pleasure. In real life both men and women like to be seduced and overwhelmed at times, but at other times it is very gratifying to be active and take the lead. Clearly, unrealistic and rigid attitudes do not lead to a satisfying love relationship for either person.

Nowadays the old, rigid gender roles are changing. I think it will always be important to be clearly male or female—as the French say, "Vive la différence"—but that does not mean that a man cannot love to cook and must never be sensitive and gentle, or that a girl should not be a great athlete or a brilliant scientist if she wants to.

Lovemaking too becomes more meaningful and pleasurable if it is shared and reciprocal and varied. The man should be liberated from the pressure of having to give a perfect performance and from never daring to admit that he also has emotional needs and that he might wish to be caressed. And the woman should certainly feel free to initiate sex when she is moved to and to experience and to actively seek her own erotic pleasure, and not to think only of pleasing her partner. The quality of life and love and sex is enhanced when both persons in a relationship are free to express and to accept each other's capabilities and the vulnerabilities as well.

Chapter 5

WHAT IS NORMAL SEX?

It is really not clear where the boundaries between normal or abnormal human sexual behavior lie. Concepts of sexual normalcy and pathology are based more on social attitudes than on scientific facts. Even now our definitions of what is sexually normal and what is abnormal is in the process of changing.

In the past people were horrified and considered "kinky" or sick any sexual practice which deviated from the straight "missionary position" of sexual intercourse. Many sexual practices which are now considered normal, such as masturbation or oral sex, were actually defined as criminal acts and there are still people serving jail sentences today for these "crimes." In the last chapter I mentioned that sexual fantasies which seem a bit unusual are not considered harmful by most authorities any longer, although in the past it was believed such fantasies were a sign of deep trouble.

Masturbation

Masturbation means stimulating your own genitals. Most males masturbate with their hand, while some rub their penis against the surface of the bed. Most females masturbate by rubbing their clitoris with their finger in a rotary motion. Some cross their legs and tighten and relax their thigh muscles rhythmically. Some people use a vibrator or a stream of water on the clitoris or penis in order to masturbate. The frequency with which people masturbate varies from several times a day to once a year, but most normal people do it sometimes. There are some gender differences in masturbatory frequency. Almost all males—95 percent—masturbate, and do so most frequently during adolescence. As a male ages, his ejaculatory needs and his tendency to masturbate decline, but masturbation is normal throughout life. Even when a partner is available, occasional masturbation is a normal phenomenon.

Kinsey found that about 40 percent of normal women masturbate. Some girls begin to masturbate during childhood and adolescence, but others do not discover that they can pleasure their own bodies until after they have had sexual experiences with a partner. So female masturbation peaks later in life, probably between the years of thirty and forty.

For a long time masturbation was considered both sinful and harmful. Some religious groups regarded masturbation as a cardinal sin. The general public, and doctors as well, believed that masturbation was extremely dangerous, causing insanity, cancer, general weakening, blindness, sterility, mental deficiency, impotence, sterility, death, and hair growth on the palm of the hand! "Cures" for masturbation included being put in a straitjacket and/or having one's clitoris surgically removed. Today we know that most normal people masturbate and that far from causing any harm, masturbation may be a constructive experience. Again, most authorities now believe that it is normal for males and females to masturbate throughout life, even when a sexual partner is available. In fact, self-stimulation can be a normal and enjoyable part of lovemaking when you do it together with a partner.

However, there are some people who masturbate compulsively and excessively. Such people are suffering from anxiety and use masturbation as a tranquilizer. Their masturbation is not what causes harm, it's their anxiety. They need help for their anxiety. Some people masturbate because they are afraid to have sex with a partner. But again, it is the fear of a partner, not the masturbation, that is the problem.

There is really only one danger from masturbation, and that is the guilt and shame that some people feel about it. If you feel guilty about masturbating, if you are in conflict about doing it, and worry about the sexual fantasies that accompany it, these negative feelings may become associated with all your sexual thoughts and feelings and that certainly is not very good for your sex life.

Sexual Fantasies

It is impossible to talk about masturbation without also mentioning sexual fantasies, because most people create erotic images in their mind while they are stimulating themselves. When a baby first fingers his genitals he is probably not thinking about anything. However as soon as our brains mature enough so we can form thoughts and images, masturbation is usually accompanied by fantasies. In other words, people tell themselves sexy stories or imagine sexual pictures or create whole erotic scenarios while they are stimulating themselves. Some people don't use their imagination, but look at erotic pictures instead. Certain magazines are devoted to providing sexual images which are often used for masturbation.

The content of sexual fantasy varies from a simple image of a nude person or of just genitals, to complicated plots which involve seductions, desert islands, heroic rescues, bondage, orgies, groups, homosexual activities, and so on. I have already mentioned that some people have sexual fantasies which seem "way out" or sick. Such fantasies may worry them, and cause them to feel that they are disturbed or make them feel guilty and ashamed. Actually, perfectly healthy and normal men and women enjoy sexual fantasies, not only during masturbation, but also when they are sharing sex with a partner. The content of the fantasy is not as important as people think. Fantasies act like a kind of tranquilizer because they distract one from momentary anxieties that may occur during lovemaking and spoil it. Thus fantasizing can enhance the sexual experience. That is why we sometimes teach patients the use of fantasy in sexual therapy.

Nocturnal Emissions

If a male does not have sufficient orgastic outlet he will experience "wet dreams" or nocturnal emissions. This means that he will have a dream with erotic content during which he will ejaculate. This is perfectly normal. In fact all healthy persons experience sexual excitement states during sleep. Sleep can be divided into two stages— quiet sleep and REM sleep. REM stands for "rapid eye movement." Scientists have discovered that four to five times during each night people's eyes move rapidly behind their closed eyelids and they dream. During these periods males experience full penile erections and females lubricate. Some women also have orgasms during sleep.

Other Sexual Practices

Apart from masturbation and sexual fantasies, which are not considered harmful—simply because most normal persons masturbate and have fantasies and are not injured thereby—the question of what is normal in sex cannot be answered with precision because there is not enough scientific data available to form reliable and valid criteria. But clinical experience has led to the opinion that certain things are definitely abnormal, while other questions remain controversial.

If a person is confused about his gender, that is considered definitely abnormal. If a person persistently or repeatedly is unable to function sexually or to enjoy sex, in other words if he feels no desire and can't have an erection or orgasm, there is something wrong and help is needed.

If a person is distressed and upset about his sexuality there is something wrong and he can use some help, if only in terms of reassurance. I also feel it to be abnormal if one cannot sustain love and intimacy with another person. Obsessions and preoccupations about sexual organs or functioning also seem to me to be pathological. And certainly irresistible sexual impulses which cause harm to the person

or to someone else, like rape for example, should be considered pathological.

There is some controversy in medical circles about whether
or not variations in sexual desire such as fetishism and homosexuality
are really abnormalities. Some people feel these attractions are not
abnormal, but are merely preferences like life-style preferences. I do
not agree with this view. I believe that while normal people may
and do have some homosexual or other variant elements, variant
sexual behavior when it is exclusive or very intense grows out of
psychological conflict. But whether one considers variant sexual desires as pathology or style, no person should be persecuted, discrimi-
nated against, or "put down" for his sexual preferences.

The human sexual experience is very flexible and a large variety
of different things excite different people. I think it would be an error
to define sexual normalcy rigidly at this time when we have incomplete scientific knowledge. I believe that any form of stimulation and
any sort of fantasy which increases the pleasure that lovers can share
is normal. If no one is harmed one should not feel guilty about such
preferences. The only time I have seen problems grow out of a person's
wish for something sexual is when his or her partner objects to it. For
example a man may desire oral sex, but his wife may be repelled
by the idea. Neither the husband who wants it, nor the wife who objects to it, is sick or wrong or should be coerced or manipulated into
doing what he or she doesn't want to do. Differences in sexual wishes
and styles should be respected. If there is a discrepancy or conflict
in sexual desires a couple will have to deal with this with the same
good sense and consideration for each other which they bring to the
resolution of other disagreements such as what to eat and where to
go on vacation.

REPRODUCTION

It seems like a miracle that one is ever born because the odds are overwhelmingly against human sperm and ovum getting together. For one, they are tiny cells that must find each other in the vast labyrinth of the female reproductive tract. Another difficulty is that these germ cells, being haploid, have a short life span and have to get together in the brief period before they die.

The reproductive physiology of males and females is different but complementary. The female produces just one ovum each month which dies 48 hours after it pops out of the ovary. Sperm live only 36 hours, and it takes millions of sperm to track down, penetrate and fertilize one ovum. Not only are many needed to penetrate the ovum, but many are lost during that long journey from the penis. Millions of sperm are constantly produced to insure an adequate fresh supply so that a male is always prepared for a sexual opportunity. It is this abundance of sperm (plus our strong sex drives which move us to copulate) that insures the survival of the species against considerable odds.

The Male Sperm

The testes (where sperm and testosterone, also called androgen, are produced) lie relatively dormant until a boy reaches puberty. Then a certain part of the brain (the hypothalamus) sends messages to the "master gland" (the pituitary), which then begins to manufacture two hormones (gonadotropins) called L.H. and F.S.H. (luteinizing hormone and follicle stimulating hormone). These hormones trigger the testicles into action and stimulate the cells of the testes to grow. It is at this point that the seminiferous tubules in the testes begin to produce adult amounts of the male hormone testosterone and sperm.

The important thing to remember about sperm is that they contain only half the number of chromosomes found in the other cells of the body. This is what makes reproductive cells.

The sperm is beautifully engineered to fulfill its function of tracking down the ovum and penetrating it. And that is quite a feat. This infinitesimal little creature has to travel incredible distances against strong currents to find that tiny egg which is hidden somewhere in that vast cosmic space of the female reproductive galaxy. It carries its crucial "pay load" of genetic material in its "head" and the rest of its substance is formed into a mobile tail which, with great energy, can propel it on long journeys against the currents of the vaginal and uterine fluids even up into the fallopian tubes and body cavity. It is also equipped with a sophisticated sensor system which enables it to find that tiny egg, and with enzymes which allow it to penetrate its formidable protective covering and so fertilize it. If a sperm does not fertilize an egg, it dies in about thirty-six hours after ejaculation. There are approximately five million sperm in each ejaculate, and if they are lucky, one of them makes it into the egg.

Testosterone, the male hormone, is produced by the Leydig cells of the testes. It is technically known as a "steroid," and is a highly interesting substance. Before birth, the tiny amount of testosterone secreted by the XY fetus six weeks after ovulation produces differen-

Sperm

This is a greatly enlarged diagram of a human sperm cell. It can be divided into a head, a neck, a middle piece, a tail, and an end piece. The head contains highly concentrated DNA, which as you remember contains half of the genetic material, or a haploid number of chromosomes, which is contributed to the offspring by the father. The head is covered at its front part by a membrane envelope called an acrosome. This envelope contains a lysing agent which dissolves the membrane that covers the egg so the sperm can penetrate. The middle piece contains mitochondria, which are those parts of a cell that provide it with energy for whatever it will do. In the case of sperm the mitochondria will energize the tail, whose movements propel the sperm through the female reproductive tract. The tail of the sperm contains bundles of protein fibers which are arranged in a neat circle, an arrangement which makes for maximum motility. A healthy male produces several million sperm each day during his reproductive years. Each ejaculate contains approximately 400 to 600 million sperm. The sperm "swim" in a fluid called semen. It consists of sperm which have traveled up through the vasa deferentia and fluids from the prostate gland and from the seminal vesicles.

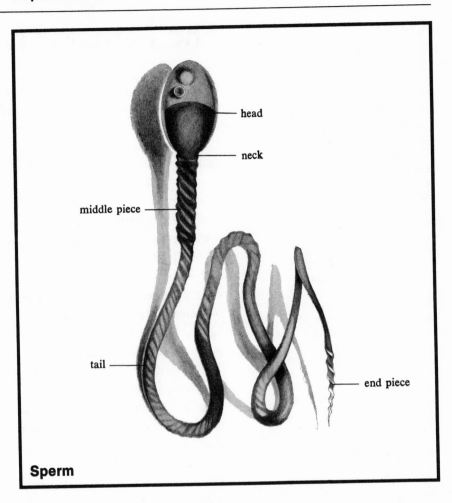

Sperm

tiation of the embryo into a male. It causes the growth and development of the testicles and the penis which are the primary sexual characteristics of the male. The sex hormone also produces the secondary sexual characteristics which differentiate males from females both physically and perhaps emotionally as well. When they are children, boys and girls look pretty much alike, but around the age of eleven to thirteen males and females begin to develop quite differently because of the action of the sex hormones. This period is called puberty and will be discussed in detail in Chapter Nine.

Ovum

This is a picture of a human ovum several hours after fertilization. You can tell it has been fertilized because of the presence of two polar bodies.

The ovum is the female reproductive cell. Like the sperm it also contains a haploid number of chromosomes, or the nucleus of the ovum contains the half of the new baby's genetic material that is contributed by the mother. In contrast to the sperm, the ovum does not travel, but remains in the female reproductive tract, and it must provide the material for the first few cell divisions that occur after fertilization and before outside material is delivered by the maternal body. The egg also must contain the energy for these early cell divisions, because the only contribution the sperm makes is the genetic material necessary for chromosome completion. For this reason the oocyte (partially mature ovum) is much larger than the sperm (85,000 times larger) and in fact is larger than most other cells in the body. For example, bird eggs are single oocytes. The mammalian egg is much smaller, but all eggs contain fats, proteins, ribosomes, RNA, and other building material which are called yolk.

The Female Ovum

One of the major differences between male and female reproductive biology is that after puberty the male's testes function steadily all his life. The seminiferous tubules are constantly producing sperm and the Leydig cells keep a steady level of testosterone flowing into the man's blood stream, bathing his brain and body with a constant environment of hormones. In contrast, female reproductive physiology is far more complex because it is organized in cycles during which the hormone level fluctuates markedly. In the human female, the cycle lasts approximately twenty-eight days.

When a female reaches puberty (which is triggered, as is the male's, by the hypothalamus), one germ cell matures every twenty-eight days and is released from the surface of the ovary. This is called ovulation. Ovulation is governed by the pituitary gland which uses L.H. and F.S.H. as its regulatory agents. All female mammals experience such a reproductive cycle, but its length is species specific. The details of the female reproductive rhythm, which is also known as the menstrual cycle, will make more sense if you recall the structure and function of the ova and of the female sex hormones described in Chapter Two. If you remember, the ovaries are two egg-shaped organs which lie inside the pelvic cavity. They were made of the same embryologic material from which the testes came. Their structure is considerably different however. While the testes contain innumerable tubules which are forever producing millions of sperm, the ovaries contain innumerable immature egg cells underneath their surface capsule which can lie dormant for as long as thirty years. In the human, only one of these ova matures and is released each month. (Sometimes two get released. If both are fertilized by a sperm, fraternal twins are produced.) The rest of the ovarian cells are similar to the cells of the testes in that they also have two functions: the production of germ cells, and the secretion of the sex hormones. The female has two sex hormones: estrogen and progesterone.

Again the important feature of the ovum, the female reproduc-

During spermatogenesis (sperm formation) four complete sperm are produced from each spermatogonium (sperm producing cell). In contrast, during oogenesis (ovum formation) all the cellular material is gathered up in one of the four daughter cells, while three of the offspring of the original oogonium (ovum producing cell) are discarded as polar bodies and shrivel and disintegrate. While it is growing, the oocyte is nourished by follicle cells which surround it as it matures in the ovary.

In the human female, oocytes begin to develop just beneath the surface of the ovary by the third fetal month. By the time of birth, about 400,000 primary oocytes are contained in the ovary. They wait patiently throughout the thirty years or so during which the woman is fertile. Each twenty-eight days, governed by the rhythmic dance of the female reproductive hormones, one of these oocytes completes its maturation. It divides, grows, discards one polar body and pops out of the surface of the ovary—full of yolk and ready to receive a sperm. After fertilization the oocyte completes its second and final meiotic division, extrudes the last polar body, and begins the process of cell division toward the creation of a new individual.

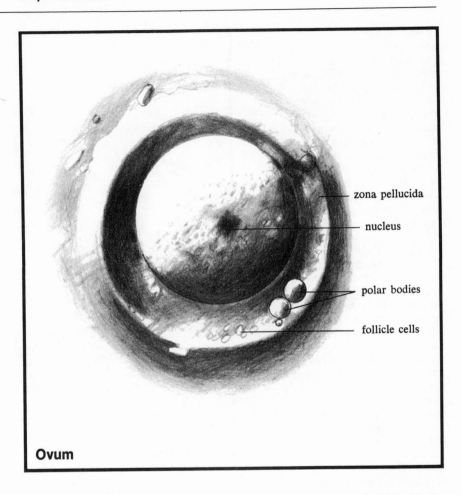

zona pellucida

nucleus

polar bodies

follicle cells

Ovum

tive cell, is that it contains only 23 chromosomes, one half of the genetic material which will shape the future offspring. In that regard it is like the male sperm. However, the engineering of the ovum is totally different from that of the sperm since its functions are so different. The ovum does not have to hunt down a sperm. It just has to sit in the right place and be attractive. Then it is either selected or it actively selects, and draws into itself, from the many, many suitor sperm which have gathered around it, the one with which it wishes to fuse or the one which is most effective in penetrating its defenses. Compared to a sperm, the human egg is enormous. It contains the

Fertilization

This diagram shows the moment of fertilization. Many sperm surround the oocyte, but only one has made its way through the zona pellucida which envelops it. The acrosome at the head of the sperm has released its lysing substance and the oocyte has developed a little bump at the point of contact and appears to draw the sperm into itself. One polar body, which consists of nuclear material discarded during the first meiotic division, lies at the periphery. After the sperm enters, the oocyte will undergo the second meiotic division during which another polar body will be extruded and discarded. Then the sperm and egg nuclei will fuse and the fertilized ovum will begin to divide and to produce a new offspring. If the egg is not fertilized, it will not undergo its second meiotic division, it will cease to be fertile, and, it will die within about twenty-four hours, after which it is re-sorbed by the woman's body.

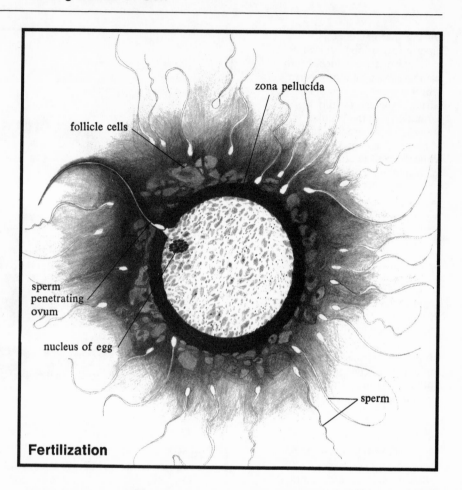

zona pellucida

follicle cells

sperm penetrating ovum

nucleus of egg

sperm

Fertilization

nourishment, energy supply, and protein building material necessary for cell division during the period just after fertilization. For when the sperm enters, the fertilized ovum, which now contains a complete set of 46 chromosomes (one half from mother and one half from father), immediately springs into action. The fertilized cell, from which the baby's entire body will be made, starts dividing rapidly. At first all the cells are alike, but a little later different cells start to differentiate. When the embryo is made up of many cells it begins to receive outside supplies from the mother's body, first through the specially prepared uterine lining and later through the placenta. The details of pregnancy are fascinating, but are beyond the scope of this book on sex.

The two female hormones produced by the ovaries are unlike testosterone in that they do *not* increase sexual desire. On the contrary, estrogen seems to have a mildly calmative effect on some persons. Estrogen affects the cells of the female genital organs and causes them to mature and remain functional. It also affects the cells of the skin, bones, and breasts and so at puberty it causes the typical female secondary sexual characteristics to develop. Progesterone is produced by the cells of the scar made by the little wound which occurs when the ovum pops up through the surface membrane of the ovary. Its function will be explained later.

The Menstrual Cycle

Menstruation has been poetically described as "the weeping of a disappointed uterus." The disappointment refers to the fact that the act of menstruation implies that the female did not become pregnant that month. We have already said that after puberty the pituitary gland secretes two gonadotropic hormones called L.H. and F.S.H. These hormones stimulate the cells of the ovaries to secrete estrogen which in turn causes one of the immature egg cells to become a mature ovum. This maturation takes about twelve days. On day twelve (or about), the ovum breaks through the capsule of the ovary. When this occurs the woman is said to "ovulate." The ovum then travels through the fallopian tubes towards the uterus. This journey takes between one and four days and during this period of time the female is fertile. This means that if she should have intercourse during this time she is very likely to become pregnant. If no fertilization occurs within forty-eight hours the egg dies.

After the egg ruptures from the surface of the ovary, it leaves a little scar which is called the "corpus luteum" (yellow body). The cells of this scar manufacture the second female sex hormone, progesterone. Progesterone causes the walls of the uterus to thicken which provides the newly fertilized egg with a place of shelter and nourishment until the mother's womb can supply it through the placenta which develops a little later. In the first few days the embryo nestles into the specially prepared lining of the uterus.

Every month progesterone causes the uterus to prepare for a possible pregnancy by building up a thick, nourishing lining of cells. This lining is richly supplied with blood. If no fertilization occurs within ten days or so, progesterone and estrogen secretion drops and this hormone withdrawal causes the uterus to shed its lining. The process can be compared to clearing a nicely set table if the expected guests don't arrive in a reasonable period of time. The lining, now shed, is carried out of the uterus through the cervix and out of the vagina. This shedding of bloody uterine lining is called menstruation. After the menses stop, the cycle begins again.

If an egg is fertilized (that is, if the woman becomes pregnant), progesterone continues to be secreted and the lining is maintained throughout the pregnancy. It is not shed and there is no period. A missed period is one of the earliest signs of pregnancy, though there are other reasons for missing a period.

Menstruation (the Menarche) generally begins between the ages of ten and eighteen. At menopause, which occurs between the ages of forty-five and fifty-five, a woman's menstrual cycles stop and she is no longer able to bear a child.

It takes about four to eight days for the uterus to shed its lining. During this time bloody fluid emerges from the vagina. Usually this is not painful, but occasionally the uterus contracts during menstruation causing menstrual cramps. These can usually be relieved by appropriate medication. Often a person's periods become less painful after the birth of a child.

In most mammalian species the female goes into "heat" during ovulation. This means that during her fertile period, a female mammal becomes extremely interested in sex and is highly receptive to the male. During heat, most mammals secrete a substance from their genitals which has an odor that evokes intense sexual desire in the male of the species. When she is not in heat, she seems to have little sexual desire. This is *not* the case with human beings. The female of our species is always interested in sex and can always be aroused, even when not in her fertile period. In fact some women feel "horniest" or most sexual around the eight days surrounding their periods. The human male is always interested in the female, even when she is not fertile.

Some women notice little or no emotional changes during the peri-menstrual period. Others may feel somewhat vulnerable and a little more irritable and sensitive; some feel more aggressive, and some even feel more creative than usual. If these feelings are intense and disturbing they can be helped by medical treatment. However, they are usually normal physiologic reactions, and if you are in touch with your feelings and can handle them, you need experience no particular psychological difficulties during these times.

One explanation of the emotional changes experienced by some women around their menstrual period is that estrogen and progesterone have calmative effects and also are an antidote for the male hormone androgen. So during her period a girl undergoes a sort of "mini-menopause" where she is under the domination of male, rather than female hormones. Let me repeat, however, that the psychologically and physically healthy female does not make a big deal out of her periods, and does not let them interfere with her normal life. If there is real emotional upset or significant pain, something is wrong and you ought to see your gynecologist.

Two kinds of devices are used by women to manage their menses: pads and tampons. Pads are simple "bandages" which are worn over the vaginal opening. They are held in place by a double-edged tape, by pins or by a beltlike device. The advantage of pads is that they are easy to use. A disadvantage is that they occasionally get displaced and bulge, which could be a source of embarrassment. Also, pads make it difficult to perform athletic activities.

Tampons are tubes of absorbent material which are placed inside the vagina where they soak up the menstrual fluid as it emerges from the uterus. A little string extends from the vaginal entrance which makes for easy removal. Tampons do not bulge, and one can swim, play tennis, ski, and the like while wearing them. There is one temporary disadvantage. For some girls, it is initially difficult to learn how to insert a tampon. Because the vagina is not part of the body image of girls, because it is internal, invisible, and largely silent, many girls do not *know* exactly where their vaginal entrance is and have difficulty finding it. Also many are timid about inserting an object into their vagina. Usually with a little practice, reassurance, and sometimes with the help of a mirror, any girl who has no physical problem can learn how to use a tampon. The process is something like learning to use contact lenses: awkward at first and then very easy.

There are some myths about menstruation as it relates to sexual and athletic activities. In some cultures a menstruating woman is considered "unclean" and must wait ten days until the last drop of blood has emerged from her vagina and then undergo a religious ritual cleansing bath before she can have intercourse with her husband. Sex may not be esthetically pleasing to some people during menstruation, but it is in no way medically harmful. In fact some women experience an increase in sexual desire around the time of their menses, and some men have no qualms about intercourse during menstruation. It is purely a matter of esthetic preference whether you want to have sex during your period or not. Similarly, despite some myths to the contrary, it is perfectly safe to engage in any sport during your period, including swimming and riding if you are comfortable.

Pregnancy

Pregnancy and childbirth can be one of the great experiences in a woman's life. It certainly was for me. This is especially true if mother and father love each other and want to raise a family together. I will not discuss the biology of gestation and childbirth here because that information is widely available. However, I do want to say a word about sex during pregnancy.

It is often important for the welfare of a couple's relationship that they continue to have sexual pleasure together during pregnancy. After all, neither the father nor the mother lose their sexual desire for the nine months of pregnancy. And luckily, intercourse and orgasm are entirely safe and harmless for mother and infant and father too during pregnancy. This is true right up to the time the amnionic "bag of water" breaks, which means labor is about to begin.

Naturally, as pregnancy advances the couple will have to use coital positions which are comfortable in the face of the mother's enlarged belly. The most common position for intercourse for non-pregnant couples is the "male superior" (or "missionary position," named after those missionaries working in pagan cultures who considered this position permissible and other positions and sexual practices sinful). In this position the woman lies on her back with her legs spread apart and the man lies on top of her with his legs between hers. Variations of the male superior positions involve different angles of the woman's legs. They may be stretched out, bent at the knees, raised up to her shoulders, or wrapped around the male's body. The male may lie flat on top of the female, rest his weight on his elbows, or raise his upper trunk and rest his weight on his hands.

In the "female superior" positions, the woman is on top. The man lies on his back while the woman straddles him. Again, there are variations of the female superior which involve different postures on the part of the woman. She may sit upright, or lie on top of the male, or assume a variety of intermediary postures.

Both these "face to face" positions are unsuitable for intercourse during advanced pregnancy. Positions where the man enters from the rear are much more comfortable. This can be done "doggy fashion," in which the female is on her hands and knees while the male enters from the rear. The "side by side" position is also suitable, where the man lies on his side behind the woman, who also lies on her side, and again, he enters her from the rear. Other positions which do not put pressure on the pregnant belly are sitting on a chair or lying on a bed while the man stands in front of her.

After the baby is born, it is considered wise to wait for about six weeks, until the mother's reproductive organs have regained their normal state, before resuming intercourse. But this does not mean

Human Reproduction

This diagram summarizes and puts together all the pieces of the reproductive process.

Sperm are formed in the seminiferous tubules of the testes, which are located in the scrotal sac. These tubules come together in the epididymis where the sperm finish their maturation. They form the sperm duct (vas deferens) which runs up to the body cavity through the inguinal canal in the groin and empties into the urethra at the base of the penis. During ejaculation the organs contract and the sperm plus fluids from the seminal vesicles and from the prostate gland collect in the posterior part of the urethra. The mixture of sperm and fluids from the male glands is called semen. The erect penis is shown inside the vagina. Ejaculation has deposited semen near the cervix or entrance to the uterus. The sperm move up through the uterus into the fallopian tube where they encounter a freshly erupted oocyte.

A mature oocyte has been lying dormant having started but not completed its first meiotic division, near the surface of the ovary since the woman was a fetus in her own mother's womb. Fourteen days before ovulation, FSH from the pituitary gland caused the oocyte to complete its first meiotic division and also caused the surrounding follicle

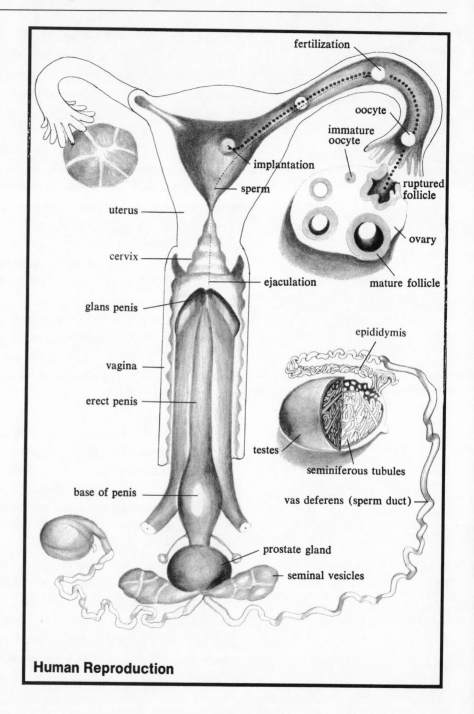

Human Reproduction

cells to form a nourishing capsule—the follicle. On day fourteen of the menstrual cycle, stimulated by increased estrogen production by the follicle cells, the pituitary sends a bolt of LH which touches the oocyte on its way. Within twenty-four hours of this event the woman had a sexual encounter which caused the male to become excited and erect, and to ejaculate approximately 400 million sperm into her reproductive tract. Incredibly some of these sperm tracked down the tiny oocyte, which was traveling down the fallopian tube. Its acrosome spilled some lysing substance into the tough egg membrane. The membrane yielded, and the egg reached out as if to welcome the sperm inside. Now it finishes its second meiotic division, rejecting the second unnecessary polar body, and the two incomplete, haploid nuclei travel to the center of the cell and join! The diploid number is again complete—genetic material has been reshuffled in the service of evolution. Within thirty hours the fertilized egg starts to divide and, still traveling, implants itself into the welcoming lining of the uterus. Nine months and many biological events later, a baby with the fused characteristics —carried on the DNA code of the chromosomes—of mother and father is born.

that sex play which does not involve penetration is contraindicated. In fact, after the birth of a new baby, a couple is apt to feel very close and physical intimacies may be especially enjoyable at this time.

Chapter 7

BIRTH CONTROL

Sex is nature's tool for procreation. We have been programmed so that our erotic urges are compelling and sex is highly enjoyable in order that we may be moved to mate and multiply. However, we have gone a bit overboard on reproduction, to the point where the number of people on earth threaten to overwhelm our food supplies and our natural resources. So in today's society, only a small proportion of sexual activity is conducted for the purpose of creating babies. Sex is most often experienced for the pleasure it provides, and also because it enhances life and deepens love. This situation has created a controversy. According to some religious viewpoints, non-procreational enjoyment of sex, especially outside of marriage, is frowned upon and even considered sinful. Other equally responsible religious groups feel that sex for pleasure and for the enhancement of life and relationships is good. All religious and moral authorities do agree, however, that sexual enjoyment should occur within the framework of humanity and responsibility. This means neither partners nor offspring should be emotionally or physically harmed by the sexual experience. Certainly one of the greatest hazards for both parents and offspring is an unwanted pregnancy or the birth of a child who is not desired by his parents. That can be a tragedy. Some solve this dilemma by deciding not to have sex until they wish to have, and are prepared to care for, a baby. Others, however, feel that sex is all right, apart from having a family. No one can make this decision for you. It is your responsibility. For those who have decided that it is O.K. to have sex apart from procreation there are many birth control methods available which permit one to experience the pleasure of sex while reducing the chances of pregnancy.

The first requirement of any contraceptive, or method of preventing conception, is that it be safe for both partners. And second, it must be effective. Also it is important that it should not interfere with sexual pleasure, nor should it be emotionally unacceptable to either. The best contraceptive would be one that, for a particular couple, provided the most protection against pregnancy, with the least interference with the sexual pleasure of both, and at the least cost and inconvenience.

Unfortunately, no contraceptive yet devised is perfect for everyone. However, there are some very good ones, and I will now describe the advantages and the disadvantages of some of the most popular ones currently in use.

Non-Mechanical Methods

Coitus interruptus is a Latin term which means "interrupted intercourse." Coitus interruptus may prevent conception if the couple have intercourse until the man reaches a point near orgasm. He then pulls his penis out of the woman and ejaculates outside.

Advantages: Inexpensive, no preparation required.

Disadvantages: May be frustrating both to the man and the woman. To make it work the man must have excellent ejaculatory control and even then a few sperm sometimes escape before ejaculation. Thus the method is fairly but not perfectly safe.

Comments: Probably too frustrating if used all the time, but excellent for occasional use when the couple is not prepared with other means. The couple should use techniques which will bring the woman to orgasm either before or after the man has come.

The rhythm method. This method is based on the concept that a woman is fertile only during the forty-eight hours after the ovum breaks through the surface of the ovary and travels down the fallopian tube and sits in the uterus before it dies. Couples using the rhythm method of contraception refrain from intercourse during this fertile period and engage in it the rest of the month. The rhythm method works very well for some couples, but not for all, since some women do not ovulate regularly. There are cases in which women have become pregnant even when they had intercourse during their menstrual periods! A new variation of the rhythm method entails examining the cervical mucus before intercourse. There are characteristic changes which occur around ovulation which indicate the "safe" and the "fertile" periods.

Advantages: Inexpensive. Does not diminish sexual pleasure.

Disadvantages: Not effective in all cases. Needs a doctor's guidance. May put pressure on the man who has to "perform" on infertile days. Disrupts the spontaneity of the sexual relationship.

Comments: Should be used only by couples who know the woman's ovulation pattern with certainty. This can be established by carefully recording the woman's daily temperature pattern, which reveals the occurrence of ovulation by a slight rise in the morning temperature, which is then followed by a slight drop, and/or by examining the cervical mucus.

Contraceptive Devices Controlled by the Male

Condom. The condom is a thin rubber sheath or bag that a man places on his erect penis before having intercourse. When he ejaculates, the semen is deposited in the bag rather than being released into the vagina.

Condom

The condom is the simplest
of all contraceptive methods.
Its only disadvantage is that it
interferes with the spontaneity
and to some extent with the
man's pleasure in the sexual
act. Notice the space that
is supposed to be left for the
semen near the tip of the penis.
If this is not done, the rubber
can break during ejaculation.
The condom is placed on
the penis after it is erect.

Vasectomy

This diagram shows where the
sperm duct or vas deferens
is cut and tied as it runs from
the testicle toward the
inguinal canal. This is a simple
surgical procedure that can
be done in a doctor's office,
but it is usually irreversible.

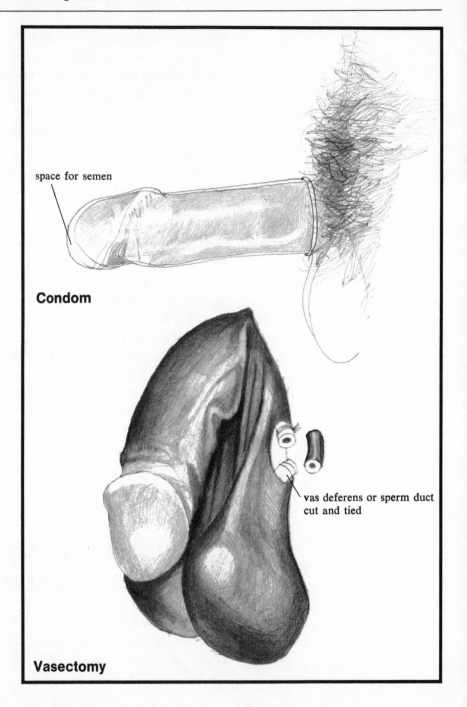

space for semen

Condom

vas deferens or sperm duct
cut and tied

Vasectomy

Advantages: Does not need a doctor's prescription; can be bought at any drugstore. Safe if put on properly—that is, with a space at the tip for receiving the ejaculate so the condom does not break. A condom also provides some protection against some venereal disease. Inexpensive.

Disadvantages: Deprives the man of sensuous pleasure during intercourse. There is also some danger that the condom may slip off the penis or have a hole in it.

Vasectomy. A vasectomy is a surgical operation that divides the vas deferens, the tube that conducts sperm to the urethra. A man who has undergone this operation has normal sexual pleasure and orgasm, but his semen does not contain sperm and therefore cannot fertilize an egg. Vasectomy is a simple procedure that can be done under local anesthetic in a doctor's office.

Advantages: Effective. Does not interfere with the sexual pleasure of either partner.

Disadvantages: There are some rare but not unheard-of medical side effects. Usually (though not always) the operation is irreversible. Some men become depressed at losing their ability to father children. Some men object to a surgical procedure.

Comments: Not appropriate for men who may wish to have children in the future.

Things to come. Scientists are now working on a male contraceptive pill. It is too early to evaluate its advantages and disadvantages.

Contraception Under Female Control

Diaphragm. The diaphragm is a rubber disk that is fitted over the "cervical os" (the entrance to the uterus) where it is a barrier to sperm that try to enter. A woman inserts the diaphragm into place through her vagina, after first filling it with a spermicidal (sperm-killing) jelly. Properly fitted, the diaphragm is not felt by either

The Diaphragm

This excellent method of contraception is sometimes not used because some women are afraid of inserting a rather large object into the vagina. Actually the diaphragm is perfectly harmless. It can cause no injury nor can it "get lost" in the body cavity. If one has trouble fitting it in, a little calm practice will usually set things right. When the diaphragm is in place the woman cannot feel it because the upper vagina has no touch sensation, nor can the man feel it during intercourse.

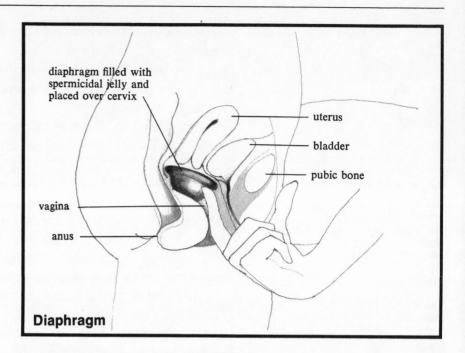

diaphragm filled with spermicidal jelly and placed over cervix

uterus

bladder

pubic bone

vagina

anus

Diaphragm

partner. It protects against pregnancy for about six to eight hours. And then it must be removed, refilled with fresh spermicidal jelly, and reinserted. After intercourse it must be left undisturbed for six to eight hours before removal.

Advantages: Relatively effective (98 percent by one estimate). Does not interfere with the sexual pleasure of either partner. Medically safe. Inexpensive.

Disadvantages: Messy. Some women find insertion of a foreign object distasteful. The jelly has a slight medicinal odor which is offensive to some people. The diaphragm must be prescribed and fitted by a physician for there are several sizes. If not properly used, this method may interfere with the spontaneity of lovemaking. Women with retroverted uteri may not find it comfortable.

Comments: In order not to interfere with spontaneous lovemaking the diaphragm must be inserted routinely even if the couple is not planning on intercourse in the next eight hours. Some gynecologists recommend the diaphragm as the safest method of contraception.

Vaginal foams, creams, and jellies. Vaginal foams, creams, and jellies consist of spermicidal material. This material kills sperm but does not harm the cells of the body. A woman inserts it into her vagina just before intercourse.

Advantages: Medical prescription not required. Some preparations also help to prevent sexually transmitted diseases.

Vaginal Foams, Creams, and Jellies

The top illustration shows how vaginal foams, creams, and jellies are inserted into the vagina with an applicator just before intercourse.

The illustration beneath it shows the mechanism of action, or just how the sperm are caught and killed by these contraceptive substances.

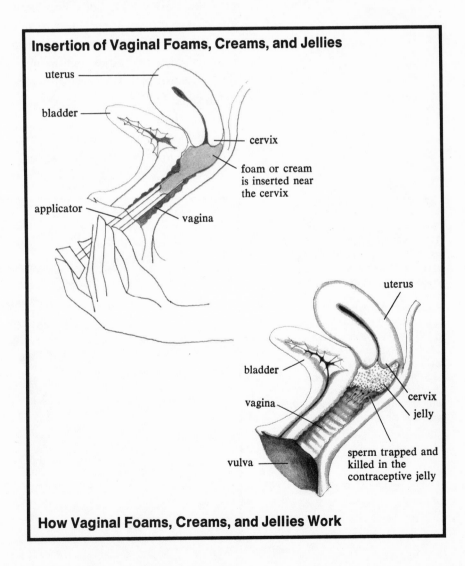

Insertion of Vaginal Foams, Creams, and Jellies

uterus

bladder

cervix

foam or cream is inserted near the cervix

applicator

vagina

uterus

bladder

vagina

cervix

jelly

vulva

sperm trapped and killed in the contraceptive jelly

How Vaginal Foams, Creams, and Jellies Work

Disadvantages: This is *not a safe method*. Also, it is inconvenient because it must be put in thirty minutes or less before intercourse and must be replaced every thirty minutes.

Intrauterine device (IUD). The intrauterine device is an ancient form of contraception. It is said that in prehistoric times women put pebbles in their uterus to prevent pregnancy. We do not know exactly how the IUD works, but it has been demonstrated that if the uterus contains a foreign object, the likelihood of pregnancy is small. Several types of IUDs are currently on the market in various shapes and made of various plastics and metals. A physician inserts the IUD into the uterus through the cervical os, leaving a thin plastic string or wire dangling into the vagina so that the woman can tell if the device is still in place.

Advantages: Relatively effective (98 percent by some estimates). Does not interfere with the sexual pleasure of either partner. No

The Intrauterine Device

This drawing shows how the IUD fits into the uterus. To insert the IUD, the physician stretches the cervix just enough to place the collapsed IUD into the uterine cavity. This hurts just a little bit for a moment. But after it is in place in the uterus (which has no touch sensations), the woman feels nothing. In fact, she can only know it is in place by checking the little filament, which hangs inside the vagina, with her finger.

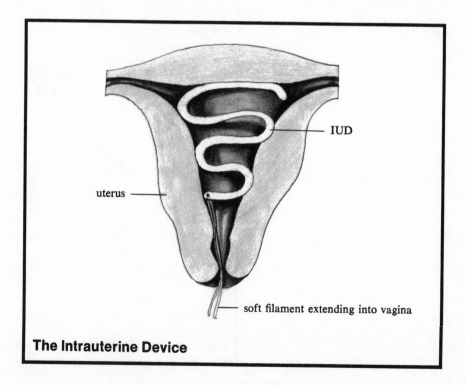

IUD

uterus

soft filament extending into vagina

The Intrauterine Device

preparation is necessary, so there is no interference with spontaneity. Inexpensive.

Disadvantages: Must be prescribed, inserted, and removed by a physician. Not all women can tolerate IUDs; a few have severe cramps and excessive bleeding. Some develop infections. Not all IUDs are medically safe. Some women object to having foreign material inside their bodies. The likelihood of genital infection is increased by the IUD.

Comments: When it is well tolerated, the IUD is the most trouble free of all contraceptive methods. However, many doctors do not recommend IUDs for young women who have not yet borne children.

The Pill. To understand how the contraceptive pill works, we must recall that the pituitary gland, which triggers the maturation of an egg in the ovary, is itself activated to start the menstrual cycle over again by the low levels of hormones in the woman's bloodstream during and around menstruation. But when a woman takes the pill, it "fools" the pituitary gland by raising the hormone levels because the pill *is* the hormone. The different types of pills consist of various mixtures of estrogen and progesterone (some also containing small quantities of androgen). Thus the pill prevents ovulation so that the woman never has a mature egg available for fertilization.

Advantages: Does not interfere with the sexual pleasure of either partner. Highly effective.

Disadvantages: Must be prescribed by a physician and requires regular physical checkups. Expensive. Must be taken every day for twenty days, then interrupted for eight days. If a person forgets to take her pill there is danger of pregnancy. Some women develop undesirable and even dangerous medical side effects. Not safe for older women.

Comments: Contraceptive pills appear to be relatively harmless for many women, but we do not yet know the long-range effects of changing the body's natural hormonal cycles. There is some reason to believe that the long term effects may be harmful to some women.

Things to come: A small sponge which is to be placed into the vagina is now being developed and tested. If it works it will block the sperm from entering the cervix, and it can also be saturated with chemicals which will reduce the dangers of contracting a sexually transmitted disease.

Tubal ligation. In the surgical procedure known as tubal ligation a woman's fallopian tubes are severed, thus preventing eggs from reaching the uterus and keeping sperm from ever reaching them. This is a relatively simple surgical procedure which can be done through the navel.

Advantages: Highly effective. Does not interfere with the sexual pleasure of either partner.

Disadvantages: Usually irreversible. Requires surgery and all surgery has some risk. Some women object to a surgical procedure. Some get depressed over the loss of their child-bearing capability.

Comments: Usually chosen by couples who have all the children

Tubal Ligation

This figure shows what happens when a woman has her "tubes tied" in order to prevent pregnancy. The operation prevents the passage of the ovum through the tube. Like vasectomy, tubal ligation is most often irreversible.

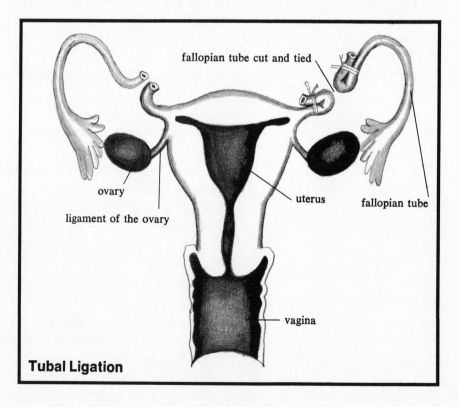

Tubal Ligation

they want. Not appropriate for women who may want children in the future.

Abortion

Abortion interrupts an unwanted pregnancy which has already occurred. People have extremely emotional attitudes toward abortion, and this subject is highly controversial. Some feel that abortion is tantamount to murdering an unborn child. And there is a logic to this opinion, for how can we decide for sure at what point an embryo becomes a human being? But others feel, just as strongly and with equal moral integrity, that a fertilized ovum or small embryo is not yet a human being, since it is merely a bit of tissue, it has no consciousness and feels no pain or distress when the pregnancy is interrupted. Rather than being concerned for this insensate creature, these people argue, we should show human concern for the woman for whom an unwanted pregnancy may constitute a real tragedy, and for the child who is entering a world where he is not wanted.

Until recently, abortion was considered a criminal act by law. Doctors who performed abortions faced the loss of their license and a jail sentence. Understandably, few doctors were willing to take such risks. Therefore, many abortions were done by unqualified persons, in secret, without anesthesia, and in dirty conditions. Many women died, sometimes in agony, and others become sterile as a result.

Today the law has changed. The courts have declared that a woman has the constitutional right to decide whether or not she wants to have a baby. Abortions are now legal in many places, and as a consequence, they are done by qualified doctors in clinics and hospitals. Abortions are now usually safe and painless.

The timing of an abortion is important. In the early stages of pregnancy it is an easy and safe procedure because in the first weeks of pregnancy the embryo is still tiny and localized, and its removal causes little discomfort or bodily disruption. However, as the embryo grows it becomes more firmly connected to the mother's body, and abortion becomes more difficult and dangerous. That is why it is so desirable to discover the unwanted pregnancy as soon as possible. One of the first signs, of course, is a missed menstrual period, though as we noted there are many other reasons why a period may be missed. The uncertainty can be removed because there are certain tests that can be performed at a very early stage by a doctor. If it is determined that a woman is indeed pregnant, and if she and her partner and her family decide that it is best to terminate the pregnancy, then it should be done at the earliest possible time, preferably in the first three months.

During the earliest stages of pregnancy, the abortion can be performed in the doctor's office. He inserts a thin tube into the uterus through which its contents are sucked out. This is not painful or dangerous. Usually a woman can go home after a short rest. After two or three weeks of pregnancy the embryo is larger and implanted more firmly in the uterine lining, requiring a larger suction tube to evacuate the uterus. Sometimes a procedure known as dilation and curettage is used at this stage. The doctor dilates the cervical opening and scrapes out the uterine lining with an instrument called a curette. This usually requires general anesthesia and is often done in a hospital. If the pregnancy is far advanced, salt solutions or a substance called prostaglandin will be injected into the uterus to start labor and end the pregnancy in this way.

An unwanted pregnancy can be emotionally painful and exhausting for both partners and their families even under the best circumstances. That is, even when the father and both families and the doctor are helpful and caring and understanding. It is really to your best interest to avoid becoming pregnant and the only way to do this, if you are going to have sex, is to realize that you can't play Russian roulette with your body. There is no such thing as, "Oh, it will probably be all right just once." We are a very fertile species and the chances are that if egg and sperm have a chance to get together they will manage to do so. If you are mature enough to have sex, whether you are male or female, you should also be mature enough to take responsibility for preventing an unwanted pregnancy.

SEXUALLY TRANSMITTED DISEASES

The message which runs throughout this book is that sex is a natural human function which we have a right to enjoy. However, sex does involve some realistic problems, and among these are the sexually transmitted diseases.

Many diseases are caused by agents such as bacteria, viruses, other microorganisms and vermin. Some diseases caused by these pests are transmitted by food. Hepatitis and food poisoning are examples of food-transmitted diseases. Some microorganisms are carried by "droplets" which are exhaled by an infected person. The common cold finds its victims through the droplet route. Many diseases are transmitted by sexual contact. Some are serious and even life threatening, others are not harmful, but merely annoying. Some can be cured, but some cannot. All can be prevented if you avoid contact with an infected person. Sex with a healthy person will never give you a sexually transmitted disease.

Some diseases are transmitted by kissing and not by actual genital contact. This should come as no surprise because saliva is mixed when two people kiss. And any microorganisms which are present in a person's mouth or even in his bloodstream will be transmitted to the person with whom a kiss is exchanged. So you will certainly be exposed to catching a cold or flu or a sore throat if you kiss a person suffering from these ailments. However, more insidious are the hidden illnesses such as mononucleosis. The viruses which cause these illnesses are contained in the infected person's saliva and so can be transmitted by a kiss. Naturally this can happen even before the person knows he or she has or is carrying the disease. The same cautions really apply to using a person's drinking glass, cigarette, or towel.

Other diseases are almost always transmitted through genital sexual contact. This is because some germs and insects are particularly adapted to living in and around the genital organs. Germs are very particular where they live. Some are found only in cheese, some only in the mouth, and some only in the genitals.

The diseases you can catch by having sex are called venereal diseases (VD) or sexually transmitted diseases (STD). Some are dangerous, some only annoying, but all of them should be attended by a physician as soon as possible.

Here are descriptions of some of the more common ones, along with their warning signs and symptoms.

Syphilis or lues. This is the most dangerous STD. It is caused by a type of bacterium known as a spirochete. Untreated, it can affect many parts of your body, causing paralysis, heart disease, blindness, insanity, and ultimately death. It can usually be successfully treated with large doses of penicillin given by a doctor. Trying to treat syphilis by taking penicillin yourself is extremely dangerous, because the wrong dose will mask the early symptoms and make you think you are cured. But inadequate treatment will not cure the disease. Several years later you will get very ill and you may die. Babies of syphilitic mothers are infected and are born with the disease.

The earliest sign of syphilis is a sore on the genitals. This will disappear even with no treatment. Later signs include fever, rash, and swollen glands.

Gonorrhea (clap). Gonorrhea is also a dangerous bacterial disease. In men it produces urethritis (infection of the urethra) and in women it causes inflammation and scarring of the internal reproductive organs which may lead to sterility (inability to have a baby). Gonorrhea may also cause blindness if it gets into the eye. It can be cured, but only with proper doses of antibiotics administered by a physician.

Early signs of gonorrhea in a man are painful urination and discharge of pus from the penis. In women, there may be no early signs. Pain in the abdomen is an advanced sign in the female.

Nonspecific Urethritis (NGU). Nonspecific urethritis is sometimes confused with gonorrhea because its first sign is also painful urination and discharge from the penis, but it is not caused by the gonoccocus, and it is not particularly harmful. It usually responds to a medicine called tetracycline.

Herpes. Genital herpes is a rapidly increasing STD. It causes painful blisters and sores on the penis and in the vagina and vulva. It is not a dangerous disease because, unlike syphilis which invades and harms other organs of the body, it stays localized in the genitals. There is some new evidence however that suggests that herpes infection may contribute to cancer of the cervix in women. It may however be very dangerous to an unborn child. If a pregnant woman has genital herpes, the child must be delivered by Caesarean section. Herpes cannot be cured as yet. The blisters clear up by themselves after a while, but they remain dormant inside the cells of your genitals and the infection tends to recur. This is a highly infectious condition. When the blisters are active or there is even redness of the genitals, you should not have sexual contact with anyone. When the condition is quiescent you are probably not infectious. Some doctors think that herpes of the mouth can be transmitted by oral-genital contact. This is an extremely painful disorder.

Trichomoniasis. Trichomoniasis is also a localized infection which is not dangerous. It is caused by tiny one-celled animals that invade the vagina and cause a discharge. In men the condition is "silent"—that is, the trichomonas organisms live in the genital tract but produce no symptoms, though the man is nevertheless infectious. Trichomoniasis can be treated with a medicine called flagil. Both partners must take this medicine or the man will reinfect the woman. Women with trichomonas have a discharge from their vagina which can have a foul odor.

Scabies. An annoying disease but not dangerous, scabies is caused by an infestation of small insects around the pubic hair. It gives rise to itching and red marks where the insects burrow into the skin around the pubic region. The cure consists of hot baths followed by applications of medication prescribed by a doctor.

There are many other STDs, including sexual warts, lymphogranuloma venereum, which is marked by swelling of the lymph glands in the groin, and sexual lice or crabs, which are lice that invade the pubic hair. But it is not necessary to know all their names and symptoms. The important thing to remember is that any sore on the genitals, any abnormal secretion from the vagina or penis, any pain in urination or sexual intercourse, or any swelling of glands around the pubic area should send you immediately to the doctor. If the doctor discovers you do have an STD, it is very important to *notify your sexual partner or partners immediately* so that they don't spread the disease to someone else, and so they can also obtain treatment, even if this causes you some understandable embarrassment.

There has been a dramatic increase in STDs recently. This is probably due to the more frequent sexual contacts between people who are strangers to each other. Doctors are now working on medications and vaccinations which will protect people against STDs, but these have not yet been perfected. The use of condoms and certain contraceptive foams that contain germicidal material offers some protection, but is not completely safe. At this time the best and really the only safe protection you have against contracting such a condition is to avoid exposure by having sex with a partner whom you know well, and who you know does not engage in sex promiscuously.

Chapter 9

THE STAGES OF HUMAN SEXUALITY

Our sexual life cycle can be divided into six stages: 1) Infancy, the period from birth to about four; 2) Early Childhood (psychoanalysts call it the oedipal period), which is considered to span the years from around four to around six; 3) Middle Childhood or "latency," which lasts approximately from six to puberty; 4) Adolescence, which ranges from puberty to adulthood; 5) Maturity; and 6) the Older Years, from menopause to the end of life.

Before these six stages can be described, it is necessary to understand that human sexuality is made up of two components: nature and nurture. In other words, our sexuality is the product of the interaction between our *biological sex drive* and our *life experiences.* Biology is constant. Every healthy person has a sex drive which is genetically determined. It is built into us exactly like the need to sleep, eat, to avoid injury, and to socialize. But experience is very variable. Some cultures and families encourage its free expression, while others regard sex, except under highly prescribed circumstances, as a cardinal sin. The sex drive is so strong that even formidable prohibitions don't abolish it entirely, but they can certainly twist and bend it out of shape.

The constancy of biology and the variability of cultural influences shape our behavior in other areas apart from sex. For example, everyone wants and needs to eat. The hunger drive is a biological constant. But nutritional habits and eating mores vary widely. In some societies people love to eat fried insects and snakes, and one-thousand-year-old eggs are considered a great delicacy which only the very rich can afford. I think we could predict your response to finding such "delicacies" on your plate at supper this evening. But you can be sure that a guest from Pakistan would similarly feel alarm and nausea if he were expected to eat a red, bloody slice of our best rare roast beef.

Our sexual drive is similarly influenced by social attitudes about sex which vary widely with culture and history. All babies have the urge to stimulate their genitals because this feels good. In some cultures such infantile masturbation is encouraged, especially for little boys, because it is considered a sign of "macho." The parents are overjoyed when he has an erection because to them this portends that he will grow into a virile and potent man capable of fathering many children. On the other hand, many other ethnic groups consider early genital activity a disaster. Childhood masturbation and signs of genital arousal are believed by many people to be medically and emotionally harmful to a youngster, and not surprisingly persons who believe this strongly discourage their children from fondling their genitals.

The same variability in social attitudes governs the expression of adolescent sexuality. In all societies, young people experience an increase in their sexual desires on a biological basis. Different societies handle this in different ways. Some expect celibacy until marriage, others are highly permissive of premarital sexual experiences.

Some of the cultures found in the South Pacific Islands, for example, encourage their adolescents to engage in premarital sexual experiences. The adults seem to take pleasure in their children's sexual expression.

Other societies have a double standard. For example, in the higher social classes of the Near East young females are strongly prohibited from having sexual contact with males. But the young male is encouraged to become sexually active. In these cultures it is felt that a male should be experienced when he marries so that he is able to teach his inexperienced bride the art of lovemaking. Other cultures, such as the high classes of India and Pakistan strictly forbid any overt sexual contact between young people. In some Oriental countries, at least until recently, marriages of upper and upper middle class families were arranged by parents for their teenage children, without regard to the bride and bridegroom's sexual attraction and preference.

Although our information about the modern People's Republic of China is not perfectly reliable, some visitors have reported that citizens, male and female, are expected to abstain from sex entirely, until their mid-twenties or early thirties, when they are expected to marry and have children. Prior to this age, they are expected to devote their energies to their country and their communities.

Many cultures have "puberty rites" to celebrate the transition between childhood and sexual maturity. Perhaps the most familiar derivative of a puberty rite in our own culture is the Jewish "Bar Mitzvah." This occurs on a boy's thirteenth birthday, and in biblical days, marked his transition from childhood to manhood. After his Bar Mitzvah a Jewish male was allowed to own property and to marry.

In our own mosaic and pluralistic society we have a great variety of sexual values. This is partly because our country is made up of peoples from a multitude of cultures which have different attitudes about sex. Also our attitudes about sex are in the process of change. We are just now coming out of a long sexual ice age, a period where sex was considered an evil force that needed to be suppressed. And we are now emerging into an era where responsible people and groups are changing these attitudes and increasingly adopting the belief that sex is a natural human function. In fact a book like this one, in which sex is discussed frankly and openly, would have been unheard of and might even have been illegal as little as twenty years ago.

It is not surprising that in this transition period there is a wide range of attitudes about sex in our own country. There are mothers who are not bothered in the least by a child's interest in sex or by his masturbation. Other equally loving mothers are horrified and discourage this strongly. They swaddle their babies so that they cannot have access to their genitals. If daughter brings her boyfriend home for Christmas vacation and wishes to share her room with him, some parents welcome this and feel proud that they have raised a sexually adequate child. Other equally caring parents feel dismayed and hurt and angry by the same request. They feel like failures as parents because they did not succeed in imbuing their child with what seems to them decent moral values and would never tolerate premarital cohabitation under the parental roof.

In an era of rapidly changing values, it is not surprising that some persons are conservative and others more open about sex. Neither are wrong or villains. We are all the products both of what we have been taught and what we have learned for ourselves. However, such wide differences in dos and don'ts can be confusing for a young person and for parents and teachers who are trying to figure out what is wrong and what is right and what is constructive and what is harmful.

Sexual Development

The human sex drive undergoes definite changes throughout the life cycle. It is with us from birth to death, but not with the same intensity. All other human functions—memory, physical stamina, eyesight, and so on—show an age-related rise and fall which is the same for males and females. Human sexuality is unique among the other biological functions, in that the sexual life cycles of males and of females, at least in our society, differ in significant respects. Babies are born with some sexual desire, but during infancy and childhood this is relatively weak. There is a tremendous increase in the sex drive for both genders during puberty which occurs between the ages of eleven to sixteen, but then sexual development takes a different path for males and females. Males experience the peak of their sexual interest and capacity during adolescence. This gradually declines as a man ages, but sexual desire and capability never disappear entirely.

Females in our society also feel a great increase of sexual desire at adolescence. However this slowly continues to increase still further and many women reach their sexual peak at around the age of forty. Then like the male, her sexual interest slowly declines but some sexual desire and a capacity can be retained into advanced old age.

Infancy

Perhaps sex begins even before birth. Some scientists feel that there are definite prenatal erections. But there is no doubt that it is present at birth. Genital responses are evident in the delivery room. Many baby boys are born with erections, and many baby girls lubricate from the first day of their lives.

Infants seem to experience pleasure and respond sexually when they are fondled and especially when their genitals are touched. Babies tend to smile and coo when their penis or clitoris is touched in the course of bathing and diapering. Baby boys often have erections when they are held and caressed. These are not learned reactions, but are part of the infant's biological heritage.

As soon as a baby can control his hands, he or she will reach for his genitals. They learn to do this because it feels good, because as we have discussed, the genitals are connected to the pleasure center of the brain. And we all learn to do what feels good, and we learn to avoid what feels bad.

These early sexual feelings are probably experienced by babies in all cultures. However parents' responses to infant sexuality vary greatly. Again, some take pleasure in their infants' sexual responses, others are distressed. No one remembers these early experiences, because the immature brain cannot yet form clear pictorial and verbal memory traces. However, emotional memories, or associations which are not consciously or verbally perceived, are established very early in life, way before language and intellectual concepts develop. And these pre-verbal associations do not simply disappear. Though we may not remember them, they are very powerful. They can shape a person's destiny by influencing his reactions all his life. That is why it is very important to handle babies with tender loving care. The way an infant's early sexual feelings are responded to by his parents can possibly influence a person's sexual attitudes for the rest of his life.

Cuddling, stroking, and other loving forms of non-genital contact between the baby and his caretakers is also believed to be important to his future emotional and sexual well being. Physical contact is very comforting and pleasurable for babies, and prepares them to love and to trust and to become sensuous persons later on in life.

Early Childhood–
The Oedipal Period

Around the age of three and four the child is well coordinated physically and has developed a definite, but as yet immature, personality. Its thinking is magical and primitive. But it can now relate to other persons and it is very much emotionally attached to its parents. All these developments affect his sexual experience.

Freud called the period between the fourth and sixth years the "oedipal period," after the Greek King Oedipus who inadvertently killed his father, married his mother, and took over the family kingdom. The gods punished him for this with blindness. What Freud meant by this was that at this stage of development, although their thinking is still immature, children are first capable of experiencing romantic feelings. Because they are living with them they are apt to become romantically attracted to the parent and sometimes siblings of the opposite sex. Of course, in the normal course of events these attractions are not expressed in sexual acts, but in wishes and fantasies—"I'm gonna marry Mommy." They "flirt," and may feel special pleasure when they do something alone with Mommy or Daddy. Romantic feelings are also evident when a child becomes angry and jealous when Mommy or Daddy pay attention to each other or to someone else or favor a sibling. Some children develop feelings of guilt about their perfectly normal romantic feelings for one parent, especially if they secretly wish that the other parent, the rival, would go away or even die. Within a loving family these oedipal feelings are usually resolved in a constructive way because, after all, it is really more realistic for a little girl to have fun with her mother, identify with her or so learn to be a woman from her rather than compete with her. In fact, in the normal course of events, a little girl will identify with her mother, that is, will try to become like her and also find and love a man of her own who will father her children. A boy also usually finds it much more gratifying to be a man like his father and join him in pleasurable activities rather than to be his rival. Instead of competing with him for mother, it is far more constructive to trust him, accept his help, and marry a girl "like the one who married dear old dad."

Although there is seldom conscious memory of these early events, they seem to be very important for later development. Some scientists consider the oedipal period a critical time in personality and sexual development. It is believed by many students of human behavior, especially by psychoanalysts, that these early family romances create the script for the drama of the romantic and sexual experiences of your entire life. These experiences determine what role you are destined to play. Are you going to be the star? The winner who carries the beautiful princess off on his white horse? In other words, will you be successful in love? Or are you destined to be an understudy, or a bit player? One who never gets a good part; one who is always the wall flower. How you feel inside is a much more important element in determining your sexual and romantic destiny than your physical appearance. And that seems to be shaped during early childhood. You may acquire some problems if your early conflicts are not resolved in a good way, but mainly this is the time you learn to love and trust and to be attracted to people who have some of the same qualities of your mother, father, sisters, and brothers: the people you loved first.

Kids continue to masturbate if they are not discouraged during this period. But while infantile masturbation is only the expression of a biological "itch," after the age of four or so it is accompanied by childish kinds of fantasies. Kids' thinking is magical and fanciful at this age and they are also very curious. Naturally this curiosity includes sex. Since very few kids get the opportunity to see lovemaking they develop childish fantasies which are often amusing. Early sexual masturbatory fantasies often entail visualizing mother or father or a neighbor in the nude or rescuing a person from danger who will then love you. Perhaps you can remember some of your own childish sexual ideas. "Sex is Daddy planting a daisy in Mommy's stomach," or "Mommy and Daddy dancing in the bedroom." My son remembers that he used to visualize a sperm as a small squirrel-like animal that would climb up the bed and into my stomach.

Occasionally, because there is little chance to check reality, kids get false and frightening ideas about sex—for example, that it is violent and harmful to Mother. This may come from as simple a thing as hearing noises in the parents' bedroom. Such ideas may cause a child to become frightened of having sexual experiences later in life.

Middle Childhood– The Latency Age

In sexually repressive societies children seem to show little interest in sex between the ages of about five and twelve. At this stage they seem to be more interested in developing their abilities in sports, gathering knowledge, and learning new skills; this is the age of hobbies and fads. Their sex drive seems to be dormant and this is why this has been called the "latency" period. But closer observation and studies of children in more permissive cultures suggest that children of this age do not only have some sexual desires but express them if they are allowed to do this. They masturbate and engage in fantasies which, though childish, are erotic. Such fantasies may include peeking at an adult who is undressed, or touching someone's genitals, or getting someone to touch theirs. When they can get away with it they also play sexual games with other children, both of the same and of the opposite sex: Mostly they just look at each other's genitals and touch them a little. Such activities are usually accompanied by a great deal of tension and laughter. They do not usually (but they may) form close romantic or sexual relationships with a member of the opposite sex. In fact, school-age children tend to form cliques or gangs made up exclusively of boys or girls, and boys and girls of this age tend to feel mutually antagonistic.

Puberty

The dramatic transformation of the child who cannot yet reproduce into the adult who is capable of reproduction is called puberty. This process begins around the age of ten and is usually finished by eighteen.

Puberty brings important physical and psychological changes. The genital organs grow and become functional so one can now have children. The secondary sexual characteristics develop and change the "unisex" child into distinctly different males and females. Sexual interest increases sharply at puberty. And we are now capable of falling in love.

As we have already discussed, all these remarkable changes are produced by the sex hormones. At around the age of ten or eleven, the "biological clock" we have all inherited turns on the gonads and now the body becomes flooded with sex hormones.

Estrogen and testosterone affect all the cells of your body to some extent, but their most dramatic effects are on the cells of the genitals and the organs which comprise our secondary sexual characteristics. The male genitals, which have not grown since birth, now reach their adult size and the testicles begin to manufacture viable sperm. The internal male reproductive organs also grow and mature.

In the female, the vulva and the internal organs of reproduction, i.e., the uterus and its adnexal structures, respond to the high levels of estrogen and they too grow and assume their adult function. The ovaries begin their monthly cycle of egg production and the young woman begins her menarche or menstrual periods which were described in Chapter Six.

Secondary Sexual Characteristics

Before puberty boys and girls look pretty much alike. But after puberty the sex hormones make us sexually dimorphic.

Homo sapiens, or human beings, are a sexually dimorphic species. This means that there are distinctive physical and perhaps even mental differences between human males and females. Not all animals are as dimorphic as we are. For example, it is difficult to tell whether a dog is a male or female. You have to check out its genitals to be sure. But there is no doubt about the gender of lions, or peafowl, because their secondary sexual characteristics are distinctive. The peacock for example has magnificent tail feathers, while the peahen is wonderfully camouflaged and plain. Male–female differences occur because certain bodily organs respond to sex hormones. We have already mentioned what happens to the genitals, but the brain and other parts of the body are also affected. In the human male the muscles, skeleton, skin, hair follicles, voice box are all responsive to androgen. Testosterone causes the human male to grow taller and have longer arms and legs and bigger hands and feet. He also develops a more prominent muscle mass which makes him stronger and faster than a female on the average. He has a deeper chest and broader shoulders than a female but a narrower pelvis. At puberty his skin becomes oily (sometimes causing acne), and the sweat glands change causing sweat to smell more strongly (this is the time when one starts using deodorants). Hair growth is affected by testosterone. The hair becomes coarser and takes on a male or a female pattern. In the male hair grows in the pubic area, on the face, under the arms and finally on the chest. The voice deepens as the larynx (voice box) enlarges.

The female sex hormone causes girls to grow less tall. The growth centers of her bones become closed off by estrogen so that a girl with the same genes for height as a boy is usually about three inches shorter than he is. Females develop a more delicate bone struc-

Sexual Dimorphism in Humans

The presence of the XY chromosome pattern causes the embryo to secrete androgens from the sixth week after conception. This fetal androgen affects the development of many organs. The reproductive and genital organs—primary sexual characteristics—are the most profoundly affected, of course. We have seen that in the absence of fetal androgen the embryonic Mullerian tissue becomes the vagina and uterus, the gonad becomes an ovary, and genital organs turn into female ones, while the Wolffian tissue degenerates. Conversely, in the presence of fetal androgen the Mullerian tissue degenerates and the Wolffian tissue develops into the internal male reproductive organs. The genitals form a penis and the gonad becomes the testes which descend into the scrotal sac.

During puberty the sex hormones create differences in other organs besides the reproductive ones. These are called secondary sexual characteristics. In the presence of a large amount of estrogen produced by the female's ovary, the growth centers of the bones close early, causing the girl to be shorter, and her hips become wider while her shoulders remain more narrow than if she had been a male with the same genetic pattern for height and skeletal form. Breasts grow and

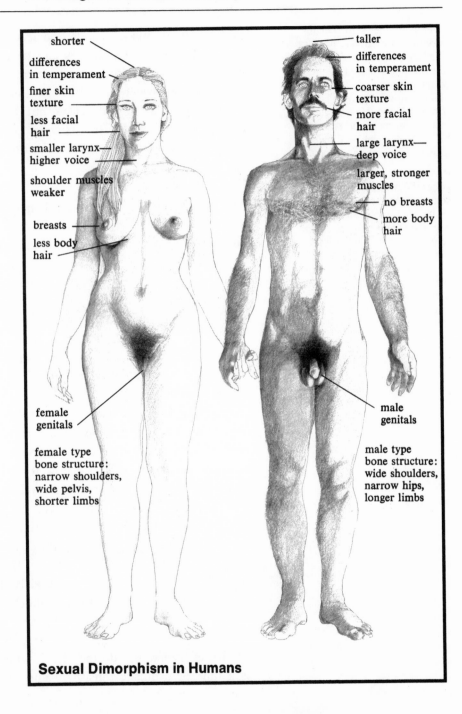

shorter

differences in temperament

finer skin texture

less facial hair

smaller larynx—higher voice

shoulder muscles weaker

breasts

less body hair

female genitals

female type bone structure: narrow shoulders, wide pelvis, shorter limbs

taller

differences in temperament

coarser skin texture

more facial hair

large larynx—deep voice

larger, stronger muscles

no breasts

more body hair

male genitals

male type bone structure: wide shoulders, narrow hips, longer limbs

Sexual Dimorphism in Humans

develop and her skin remains smooth and relatively hairless. The large amounts of testosterone secreted by the pubescent male testes cause him to grow taller with larger, stronger limbs. His muscles increase in mass and strength, his voice deepens, and hair grows on his face and body.

Perhaps the sex hormones also affect the brain. There is some evidence to suggest that males are biologically more aggressive and energetic than females, but it is difficult to tell for sure if this is due to hormones or to our culture, which encourages males to be more competitive and aggressive than females.

ture and have smaller hands and feet. Their shoulders are narrower and their pelvis wider so they can bear children. The female skin is more delicate but also becomes more oily than it was during childhood, and her sweat secretions also assume the adult odor at puberty. Pubic and axillary hair develops, but the rest of the female body is not as hirsute as the male. Breasts develop and hips accumulate fat tissue as the female figure is sculptured by estrogen, the chemical tool.

Behavior

The sex hormones also affect behavior, mainly by the action of testosterone on the brain's sex centers and circuits. Prepubescent children have sexual feelings, but these are relatively weak. The tremendous increase in testosterone, which is secreted by the testes after puberty, causes a male to become interested in sex and to desire sexual experiences. This is called libido.

Female libido also increases at puberty and this is also produced by the action of testosterone on the sex center. Females have no testes, of course, but their adrenal glands and ovaries produce a small amount of testosterone which is necessary and sufficient for female sexual desire.

Finally puberty is the time you start falling in love. Young children are not as a rule interested in a romantic relationship. The search for a mate begins in pair-bonding animals at puberty. For humans this means that one now forms "crushes." It is at this time one is apt to become interested in and attracted to one special person and that relationship becomes a central part of one's life.

In our society girls are, as a group, somewhat more interested in romantic relationships. Boys tend, as a whole, to be more interested in the physical expression of sex. But these patterns are only general; many boys fall in love and many girls enjoy sexual fun with several partners. Falling in love, loving, and being loved is one of the most important experiences in life, and more will be said about love later.

The physical changes of puberty do not take place at the same age for everyone, nor do they tend to take place evenly. Adolescence is a time of exquisite sensitivity and insecurity for most of us, and these uniquenesses can cause concern and embarrassment. Some boys' voices deepen at thirteen while others are still high pitched at fifteen. In the locker room a fourteen-year-old boy whose penis is still child-sized and has only down on his pubic region may feel very worried when he notices that his friend of the same age has a bush of coarse, pubic hair curled around the base of a fine adult-size penis. Some little girls of eleven have to contend with the embarrassment of growing breasts while others are still unhappily flat-chested at fourteen. Add to this uneven growth spurts, weight changes, and acne pimples—all at a time when one becomes very concerned about physical appearance and attractiveness.

Unevenness in development is normal and is usually resolved by the time you are seventeen or eighteen. But there are endocrine disturbances which cause truly delayed menstruation, growth, and development. These can usually be treated medically. So if you are very worried, and really far behind or ahead of your peers in sexual development, it might be wise to have your doctor check you over.

Adolescence

The period between puberty and the attainment of adulthood is called adolescence. At this time you detach yourself somewhat from your parents and seek emotional connections with your peers. Adolescence is a period of crisis. The Chinese symbol for crisis is a combination of the sign for opportunity and the sign for risk. And indeed that is a very wise way of looking at adolescence. It is a time of great opportunity: to make constructive choices about your career, life style, identity, values, and aspirations, and it is also a time of considerable risk: the risk of disappointment, vulnerability, and hurt. We will not discuss all the complexities of adolescence here, but will focus on the romantic and sexual aspects.

There are normal individual differences in sex drive. Sex is much more important to some people than to others. But during puberty every healthy person's libido becomes very much stronger than it was during childhood. The high doses of testosterone activated your sex centers. *How* this new sex drive is expressed and experienced depends on your early experiences, your personality, the expectations of your family and society, on the opportunities that are available to you, and also by the expectations of your peer group. Thus there is a great variety in how and how much young people express their sexual desires.

Some young people suppress their sexual feelings entirely, but that is rare. Most adolescents feel some romantic feelings, often for a particular person. They may experience those feelings only in day dreams or fantasy. These may be accompanied by masturbation, which, as we have previously discussed, is entirely normal. If a person is shy and should happen to be in the presence of the object of his affections, he may become so tense that he is rendered speechless and clumsy and for that reason may actively avoid contact with his love object. Other young people do not avoid contact with the opposite sex, and in fact even seek it actively. They will arrange parties, which now include boys and girls, and devise other activities, which usually first involve groups and cliques of boys and girls and later progress to things which can be shared on a one to one basis.

How much actual sexual activity goes on is very variable among normal young people. Physically, one is capable of feeling desire, becoming aroused (erect or lubricated), and having orgasms. Sometimes a young person is initiated into sexuality by an older and experienced person. But in our society young persons usually learn to be sexual with people of their own age and experience and approach a full sexual relationship in gradual stages. Some young persons elect to abstain from sexual intercourse until they are married, and some do not. But most do allow themselves various degrees of erotic pleasure even if they do not have complete intercourse.

Some young people confine their sexual activity to dating, hand holding, and kissing. These activities seem "innocent" but can be very arousing. Others proceed to foreplay or "making out," that is, they will kiss and caress each other for long periods of time. This activity will produce the excitement phase of the sexual response, in other words the men will erect and the women will get wet. Some young people then proceed to the orgasm phase. They will stimulate each other's genitals to the point of orgasm but initially this usually occurs without sexual intercourse or penetration. Again, some people remain celibate before marriage or at least until they make a serious commitment to another person, and some feel free to have sexual intercourse before this time.

In the past there was a double standard of sexual behavior in the upper classes of our society. Young males were expected to have premarital sexual experiences while females were expected to remain virgins until marriage. Since for every male who has sex a female does also, the double standard was made possible only because males would have premarital sex with females of a lower social class or with prostitutes or with those relatively few girls of their own class who were willing to have sex with a large number of partners. But the double standard appears to be in the process of changing and more young women now seem to be engaging in premarital sexual experiences with their social peers.

Becoming Coupled

So far we have been talking only about the physical aspect of sex, but puberty also ushers in our "pair-bonding" behavior, which in the human species is called love. Love can make you feel wonderful when it is returned, but miserable when rejected. And the yearning for love, or the wish to find a romantic relationship becomes a very important part of life for the adolescent. More will be said about love in the last chapter of this book.

Before puberty a child is not interested in romance and in finding a mate. He doesn't worry very much about what he looks like or what he wears. But during the adolescent years being popular and "making it" with the opposite sex becomes crucial. Physical appearance, looking good, and "personality" become a matter of intense concern.

Suddenly the way your hair looks, whether your acne pimples are visible, whether your clothes are O.K., whether your nose is the right shape, whether you are too fat or too thin become matters of life and death. It is great to learn that you are attractive and a sexually desirable person. But it is terribly painful to feel unattractive or undesirable. Feelings of rejection during the vulnerable adolescent years can leave emotional scars on one's self-esteem which a person may remember all his life.

A book can't give anyone a sure-fire antidote for adolescent growing pains. Everyone has to go through them. Just do your best to remember that you are a whole person with many valuable emotional and intellectual assets and interests, apart from just being a sex object. If you don't allow yourself to become obsessed with sex and with popularity, and concentrate on other positive aspects of yourself, you will have a much better chance of eventually developing a happy romantic relationship.

Maturity

When a person is sexually mature, he or she enjoys sex and has no shame, guilt, or anxiety about sex. Sex becomes a pleasure. The mature adult has confidence in his or her ability to function, to enjoy, and to give pleasure to the partner. But there is no compulsion to have sex. A mature person is relaxed about sex, he does not have to "prove" himself. He is in charge of his own life including his sex life. It just becomes a natural and enjoyable part of life. A mature person has a good sexual image of himself and herself. During maturity you lose your insecurities and gain a realistic view of yourself as a sexually competent male or female. Many authorities believe, and I agree, that sexual maturity goes beyond good genital functioning. The mature person prefers to be coupled to being single and maturity includes the ability to form a stable emotionally satisfying relationship with another person, with whom many things are shared, in a humanistic open way, including sex. The ability to give and to receive love is an important ingredient of sexual maturity.

Another aspect of mature sexuality in its broadest sense is being a parent. Although some persons elect not to have children, for the vast majority the experience of having and rearing children is one of the most gratifying aspects of life.

The Female Menopause and Beyond—The Older Years

Between the ages of forty-five and fifty-five the menstrual cycle ceases and a woman no longer can have children. The ovaries not only stop releasing eggs, but reduce their production of the female hormones, estrogen and progesterone. Just as the increase of sex hormones in puberty produces physical and emotional changes, the decrease at menopause also has its consequences. The reduction in hormone production affects the body of the post-menopausal woman in various ways. The woman's skin tone changes and she may develop wrinkles. The fat distribution of her body tends to change her shape so that she looks more mature. For example, fat deposits tend to accumulate around the back of her neck while her hips may slim down, and her breast tissue becomes less firm and is replaced with fat. The skin which lines her vagina may become thin and less able to lubricate. Some women also experience "hot flashes," feel warm and sweaty, because the pituitary hormones increase when the ovarian hormones diminish. Finally, some women feel emotional changes during the menopausal years. They may become more emotionally reactive and irritable and depressed.

But menopause need not be a depressing or upsetting experience. On the contrary, this can be a highly creative and joyful period in a woman's life. First the physical changes are not necessarily unattractive. If an older woman keeps in good physical condition and retains her vitality and warmth, many persons will find her attractive and desirable. The atrophic changes in her vagina can be minimized if she maintains an active sex life. Women who remain sexually active continue to lubricate and respond sexually into advanced old age. Like

men, if they "use it, they won't lose it." In fact, postmenopausal
women often experience an *increased* interest in sex! Sexual desire becomes stronger during this period for several reasons. First, pregnancy
is no longer a worry. Also the woman has had plenty of time to get
rid of her old inhibitions, and finally, while her estrogen and progesterone diminish after menopause, her testosterone doesn't. And as
you remember, testosterone (also called androgen) is the libido hormone. Also, the mature woman is likely to have learned to become a
more skillful and open lover. She may be more understanding and
sensitive to the man, who is also aging. And she may therefore be an
excellent sexual partner. For these reasons, if she has an interesting
and interested partner the menopausal and postmenopausal years can
be the best sexual time of a woman's life. Finally, if the menopausal
symptoms become truly troublesome, hormones, specifically estrogen,
can be replaced. There are some advantages and some dangers associated with hormone replacement, and the topic has producd controversy
among physicians.

The emotional ups and downs which some women experience
around the menopause have some physical as well as some emotional
reasons. Estrogen has a calmative effect on the brain and its withdrawal can make a person more vulnerable and emotional. Estrogen
and progesterone are also low during the eight days surrounding
the menstrual period in younger women, creating a "mini-menopause"
that even teenagers may experience as emotionally difficult. However
the largest contribution to the depression and upset which sometimes trouble the older woman is psychological. Many women become
upset and depressed in menopause because they fear they will be
rejected by their younger friends or their husband. If they are single,
they fear that they will not be able to find a new partner. They have
lost their child-bearing ability. If they have children, they are usually
quite grown and no longer in need of their mother's constant attention. This can leave the menopausal mother feeling unwanted.

However, just as sex can be great after menopause, if a woman
takes a positive attitude, the rest of her life can be great as well. If a
woman has developed interests apart from her family, if she has not

let her entire sense of self-esteem rest on her physical attractiveness, if she is a "real person," and if she has a good, trusting, and caring relationship with her husband, then she probably won't get into menopausal trouble. Women who are creative, involved in life, and feel good about themselves as human beings, may find the maturing of their children a relief, rather than a loss. This is not to say that career women or busy women love their children less. They are simply not as emotionally dependent on caring for them.

In short, if a woman does not believe that the menopause will leave her a depressed, cranky old lady, it won't. The "horror" of menopause is often a self-fulfilling prophecy. What she needs is to be busy and involved, to have an interesting and interested partner, and good medical management of any physical or mental symptoms that may develop.

The Male Menopause

There is no male menopause in the sense that the sex glands stop functioning at a specific age. Older men can still father children because their testes remain active, producing sperm as long as they live. In their fifties, however, testosterone production may decrease and this will produce physical and emotional problems which are somewhat similar to those experienced by the menopausal woman. Often there is some decline in sex drive, and an elderly man may experience signs of emotional instability. This syndrome has been called the male menopause or climacteric.

Although age never extinguishes a man's ability to be aroused by an attractive partner or stimulating situation, it does reduce his interest in sex, the amount of time he spends in sexual fantasy, and the urgency he feels for orgasm. As noted in Chapter Three, his refractory period becomes longer, and so does the time he needs to get an erection. By contrast with a boy in his teens, for whom erection is almost instantaneous, older men may require several minutes of tactile stimulation of the penis before it will erect. This does not detract from the pleasure a man gets from sex, however, or from his attractiveness as a partner. A physically healthy man can enjoy good sex and give sexual enjoyment up to the very end of his life.

If a person does not understand the aging process, he and his partner might worry about changes which are really normal, and this worry might be damaging to their relationship. A man who only needs a little more time and stimulation before he erects might feel, "I am too old for sex," and therefore avoid sexual activity. The wife of a man whose sex drive has diminished a little, so that he now feels moved to make love only once a week, might be hurt if she mistakes this normal diminution as a sign that she has become less attractive to her husband.

If an older couple understands the normal aging process, they can adjust their lovemaking techniques to accommodate his greater need for stimulation and lowered frequency. With love and sensitivity to changing needs, a couple can enjoy a romantic and sexual relationship until the end of life.

LOVE AND SEX

A variety of mating patterns are found among the animal species. These behavioral tendencies are inherited, not learned. Human beings also have biologic mating patterns but we don't really know what they are. For instance some apes, cows, and sheep are entirely promiscuous. All males who get the opportunity to will have intercourse with any female who is in "heat" (sexually receptive). Other animal species such as geese, eagles, and wolves, for example, will have sex only with their mates. In fact some are so monogamous that if their mate dies, they will never have sex again. Other animals are serially monogamous and will be "faithful" to one individual for a specific period of time and then leave and find a new partner. Again it is not clear what the biological mating pattern of homo sapiens would be if we were entirely free of social, cultural, and economic pressures. Would we form a bond with—i.e., fall in love with—one person until death do us part? Would we swing? That is mate with whomever was enticing and willing? Would we live with and make love to one person for several years, then lose interest, get divorced, and find someone else who would give us that thrill of a new romance for a while again?

The social and economic forces which have shaped our marriage and family patterns are so complicated that we really can't tell for sure, but there is good reason to believe that human beings are biologically programmed to be pair-bonders. Most of us are monogamous—that is, we seem to prefer sharing life with one partner over a long period of time. True, some persons seem to go through a period of sexual experimentation during childhood and adolescence, but when mature, most of us are most comfortable and happy if we are fortunate enough to find one partner with whom we fall in love and form a lasting, mutually caring, and secure love relationship. It feels good to be communicative and share with that partner on many levels. Sex within the context of such a mature, intimate love relationship is a truly beautiful experience.

There are, to be sure, some apparently normal and happy persons who enjoy "recreational sex"—sexual experiences for the pure fun of it, with no emotional commitment to any of their many partners. But psychiatrists tend to regard people who never experience a successful long-term love relationship as inhibited in love or suffering from a neurotic fear of intimacy, and I personally tend to agree. A mutually satisfying intimate love relationship makes sex an infinitely joyful and enriching experience, and even more important, sharing life with someone you love is a source of happiness and tranquillity and brings out the best and most creative aspects of both partners. People who enjoy a good romantic relationship even have less illness and tend to live longer!

The Experience of Loving

Love is an intense and profound experience which can become the center of one's life. When you are in love, your perceptions change. You tend to undervalue yourself and to overvalue your lover. You see your lover as the most wonderful, marvelous, beautiful, attractive, special, etc., etc., etc., person in the world. When in his presence you feel strong emotion—you are high. Your heart beats faster, you feel elated, you feel stronger, quicker, and infinitely more sensuous and sexual. You are at peace when you are together, and restless or in agony when you are apart. His well-being and needs come first, yours are not even noticed. Nothing is too much trouble if it is for him. You would move mountains for him. Your security vanishes. No gift you select is good enough. It is too expensive, or too cheap, too gaudy or too plain. You never look exactly right when you see him. You look too fat or too scrawny. The jeans are too tight or too loose. Your hair is too short or too long. That pimple is suddenly one square foot in diameter.

And sex is incredible when you are in love. A kiss can bring you close to orgasm. All that advice about long foreplay is nonsense. A mere telephone call can make you lubricate.

And jealousy may reach paranoid dimensions. "I called all night and she was out. I'm sure she was making out with Tom." Actually she was visiting her grandmother.

After a while the intensity diminishes. Then your perceptions of yourself and your lover become more realistic again. And when that happens you may discover that your love was based on mere physical infatuation, and that there is in reality little basis for a real mutually satisfying relationship. Then you just lose interest. However, you may discover the opposite, that the two of you are intellectually and emotionally meant for each other. Then, and if your feelings are reciprocated, a long-lasting beautiful, peaceful, and intimate caring relationship can develop. The agony of uncertainty gives way to a lovely easy peace and security. Experiences take on more meaning when you can share them and get a caring and understanding response. You are exquisitely attuned to each other's thoughts and feelings. You can count on each other to give and to be there when you need each other. You trust each other not to invade the other's vulnerabilities.

Unfortunately love can be one sided. And then it can be very painful. But a healthy person, who feels good about himself doesn't get stuck in unrequited love for long periods of time. You try your best, if there is no response, "there are other fish in the sea."

Some people think that sex becomes boring and colorless in a long-lasting relationship. I do not believe that this is true unless that relationship is not a really good one. Sex does lose its appeal if hostilities and power struggles invade the relationship. True, the first intense, flaming passion cools down a bit with time in any relationship. But sex can get even better as a couple develops increasing intimacy, as they communicate on an authentic level and find emotional and intellectual points of contact. They get to know how to please each other, they can trust and depend on each other, and it is a relief to get rid of the anxieties and hassles which burden any new relationship.

Recently society has placed too much emphasis on genitals. The mechanics of sex are important, of course, but that is the easy part of romance. The capacity for caring, intimacy, and love, which is more difficult to achieve, is a far more significant element of your life.

INDEX